Selenium Design Patterns and Best Practices

Build a powerful, stable, and automated test suite using Selenium WebDriver

Dima Kovalenko

[PACKT] open source
PUBLISHING   community experience distilled

BIRMINGHAM - MUMBAI

Selenium Design Patterns and Best Practices

First published: September 2014

Production reference: 1170914

Published by Packt Publishing Ltd.
Livery Place
35 Livery Street
Birmingham B3 2PB, UK.

ISBN 978-1-78398-270-7

www.packtpub.com

Cover image by Jeremy Segal (info@jsegalphoto.com)

Credits

Author

Dima Kovalenko

Reviewers

Anuj Chaudhary

Dave Haeffner

Dave Hunt

Alex Kogon

Commissioning Editor

Usha Iyer

Acquisition Editor

Llewellyn Rozario

Content Development Editor

Priya Singh

Technical Editor

Shiny Poojary

Copy Editors

Roshni Banerjee

Adithi Shetty

Project Coordinators

Judie Jose

Swati Kumari

Proofreaders

Simran Bhogal

Maria Gould

Ameesha Green

Indexers

Monica Ajmera Mehta

Rekha Nair

Priya Sane

Production Coordinator

Kyle Albuquerque

Cover Work

Kyle Albuquerque

Foreword

"But wouldn't we be much more efficient if we could just record our tests and play them back?" Chris, the QA manager, stood at my desk looking for confirmation.

I recall my mouth actually hanging open for a moment, then stammering something like, "What the...I don't even...Wait, what?"

I was working for a small company that produced off-the-shelf software for small- to medium-sized businesses. As part of the product line, it had a client-server desktop application, which also featured a web portal. I had spent the previous couple of years working with a small team of colleagues to create a successful automated testing framework for the desktop application. We built it from the ground up and automated a significant portion of the testing of the desktop application with it. We had intentionally left the testing of the web portal to be done manually, with the intention to automate it later. The company had also recently purchased another company that provided a web-only product intended for use by larger enterprise customers. With the purchase of the other company, automating the tests for the web products was becoming more important.

Additionally, we'd already gone through the process of tool evaluation for the automated testing of the web products. We knew that as a small company, we didn't have a huge budget to purchase expensive commercial testing tools. In fact, the budget was nonexistent; we'd have to make do with tools that were free or nearly so, and wire them together ourselves. Given that both web products supported multiple browsers, we had landed on Selenium as our solution, specifically choosing the newer WebDriver API over the older remote control API.

Mistakenly taking my apparent confusion for his having interrupted me from a tricky bit of coding, Chris pressed on to explain, "I mean, you've done great on the desktop application, but as you said, you need to be a programmer to effectively use those tests. That's great for you and Barbara because you've been working on the framework and understand how to code. The new guy, Derek, has some skills there too, and he's been able to use it pretty well. However, that kind of leaves out Cindy, Josh, and Brian. Wouldn't it be great if we could just use the Selenium IDE to record those test for the websites? Then, they could get automated tests into the suite too. We could even get Christian, the business analyst, in on it too!" Just like that, we'd started down a path; one that you may have started down yourself.

Dima Kovalenko's approach discusses problems that nearly every Selenium user has encountered at one time or another. His knowledge of the subject is born from years of experience, and that hard-won knowledge is now available to you in this very volume. By applying the patterns found here, you can navigate your way to efficient solutions to those problems. Additionally, Dima's writing style uses consistent examples throughout, and the language is engaging and easy to follow.

I envy you, dear reader. Douglas Adams, author of *The Hitchhiker's Guide to the Galaxy*, once wrote, "Human beings, who are almost unique in having the ability to learn from the experience of others, are also remarkable for their apparent disinclination to do so." If we had a book like this in the situation I described earlier, our Selenium implementation would have been much smoother. Whether you're reading this because you are looking to acquire more knowledge about Selenium on your own, or whether you've been told to use Selenium by someone else, you now have the opportunity to benefit from the experiences of those who have gone before. Seize that opportunity and enjoy working with Selenium.

Jim Evans

Core contributor to the WebDriver project, musician, and devoted husband and father

About the Author

Dima Kovalenko started his career in 2003 as a quality assurance intern during his summer internship at Rosetta Stone. Since then, he has spent many years testing software in both a manual and automated fashion in companies such as ThoughtWorks, Groupon, and many others. He has participated in many different types of projects, including language-learning software, web e-commerce stores, and legacy maintenance for telecommunication and airline companies. His experience includes support to Ruby, Java, iOS, Android, and PHP projects as an automated tester and software developer.

His first real experience with computers was at the age of 14, shortly after moving to the United States of America from Russia; this encounter has sparked a lifelong passion for technology.

Acknowledgments

This book would not exist without the help and support of the people in my life, who supported and encouraged this passion to grow and develop further. I'd like to thank my wife, Lena Kovalenko, for tolerating and putting up with my neediness and endless torrent of useless trivia. Without her support, and my constant desire to impress her, I would not have taken any rewarding risks in my career. I would also like to thank my parents Nikolay and Svetlana Kovalenko for letting my brother, Vadim, and me learn from our own mistakes and have ample computer time, that is, after the dishes were washed, naturally.

I'd like to thank my family and friends who were supportive in this project and helped me: Lil Kovalenko, Vadim Kovalenko, David Tolley, Steve Fournier II (Steve-o, formally known as "Scuba Steve"), Josiah Weaver, and Alfredo Velasquez.

This book would not be accurate without the help of Alex Kogon, Dave Haeffner, Dave Hunt, and Anuj Chaudhary. Thank you all for considering all of my insane ideas and theories and giving me good feedback.

I'd like to thank Seth Lochen, Andy Duncan, Shinji Kuwayama, and Virgil Bistriceanu for being incredible managers who encouraged me to learn new skills and grow to be a better person.

Finally, I'd like to also thank my coworkers, from whom I've learned more programming skills than any book could have ever taught me: Scott Muc, Isa Goksu, Jack Calzaretta, Surya Gaddipati, Michael Standley, Valdis Vitayaudom, Gregory Blike, Jason Lantz, and Greg Smith.

About the Reviewers

Anuj Chaudhary is a software engineer who enjoys working on software testing and automation. He has vast experience in different testing methodologies such as manual testing, automated testing, performance testing, and security testing. He has worked as an individual contributor and technical lead on various software projects dealing with all stages of the application development life cycle.

He has been awarded Microsoft MVP two times in a row. He also blogs at www.anujchaudhary.com.

He has also reviewed the book *Selenium WebDriver Practical Guide, Satya Avasarala, Packt Publishing*.

I would like to thank my wife, Renu, for always supporting me. I wouldn't have been able to spend extra hours on reviewing this book without her support.

Dave Haeffner is the writer of *Elemental Selenium* (http://elementalselenium.com)—a free, once-a-week Selenium tip newsletter that's read by thousands of testing professionals. He's also the creator and maintainer of ChemistryKit (https://github.com/chemistrykit), an open source Selenium framework, and the author of *The Selenium Guidebook* (http://seleniumguidebook.com). He's helped numerous companies successfully implement automated acceptance testing, including The Motley Fool, ManTech International, Sittercity, and Animoto. He's also the founder/co-organizer of Selenium Hangout and has spoken at numerous conferences and meetings about automated acceptance testing.

Dave Hunt lives in Kent, UK, with his wife and two sons. He has always had a passion for turning mundane tasks into one-click solutions, and when he discovered Selenium back in 2005, his career in software testing and automation development was sealed. He works from home for Mozilla, where he assists teams to create automated tests for their projects — ranging from Mozilla's web properties to the Firefox web browser and the Firefox OS mobile operating system.

Alex Kogon started programming in 1979 and has been working as an IT professional since 1985, helping small and large companies define and implement business software solutions. He has worked as everything from a Unix Systems Administrator and software tester to Internet start-up company CTO and has been a part of the senior management in a major global Investment Bank.

Since the late 1990s, Alex has been a major proponent of methodologies to improve the design and development of software, leveraging RAD techniques and developing his own pre-Agile methodologies to deliver projects to major global financial institutions in a fraction of the regular time. He now works as a Management Consultant helping organizations leverage Agile methodologies to be more efficient and effective through communication, collaboration, tools, automated testing, continuous integration, coding standards, and pair programming.

His ideas have been published in the Financial Times and Wall Street Journal and his seminal research on Additive Synthesis of Digital Signals is published and referred to frequently in research documents. Alex is currently working on a book on how to save money and improve results in corporate IT with Agile Methodologies.

I'd like to thank Ben and Tilda for providing a counterpoint in my life.

www.PacktPub.com

Support files, eBooks, discount offers, and more

You might want to visit www.PacktPub.com for support files and downloads related to your book.

Did you know that Packt offers eBook versions of every book published, with PDF and ePub files available? You can upgrade to the eBook version at www.PacktPub.com and as a print book customer, you are entitled to a discount on the eBook copy. Get in touch with us at service@packtpub.com for more details.

At www.PacktPub.com, you can also read a collection of free technical articles, sign up for a range of free newsletters and receive exclusive discounts and offers on Packt books and eBooks.

http://PacktLib.PacktPub.com

Do you need instant solutions to your IT questions? PacktLib is Packt's online digital book library. Here, you can access, read and search across Packt's entire library of books.

Why subscribe?

- Fully searchable across every book published by Packt
- Copy and paste, print and bookmark content
- On demand and accessible via web browser

Free access for Packt account holders

If you have an account with Packt at www.PacktPub.com, you can use this to access PacktLib today and view nine entirely free books. Simply use your login credentials for immediate access.

Table of Contents

Preface

Selenium Design Patterns and Best Practices will help you write better tests!

It does not matter whether you are writing a Selenium WebDriver test to test your website or shell scripts to test the HTTP API of the backend services of your multibillion dollar enterprise application. This book is not purely theoretical work, but comes from years of experience of the author and his colleagues. A lot of the practices and ideas written in this book did not appear as soon as we started to test the software. Instead, they came from years of mistakes, frustrations, and slow but continuous improvement. We do not believe that the examples and topics described in this book are definitive and static solutions to every single problem that you may encounter in your career. Instead, this book shows you some very generic solutions to very common problems that we, an ever-growing community of automated software testers, have encountered. We hope that this book will not only provide quick fixes to the problem(s) you may encounter, but will also empower you to solve more and more complex problems in your career by showing you some very simple improvement techniques.

What this book covers

Chapter 1, Writing the First Test, will guide us through the process of writing a simple Selenium test and converting it to a programming language.

Chapter 2, The Spaghetti Pattern, will help us write our second test that will completely depend on the test we wrote in the first chapter. We will understand why having tests that completely depend on each other is a bad practice.

Chapter 3, Refactoring Tests, will fix some of the pitfalls and common mistakes we encountered so far. This chapter will concentrate on the introduction of good computer programming practices such as code reuse.

Chapter 4, Data-driven Testing, will guide us through making some initial improvements to your test suite, and it will eventually prepare us to examine one of the most difficult problems in software testing: test data.

Chapter 5, Stabilizing the Tests, will help us understand that writing tests alone is not enough. We will dedicate this chapter to making our test bug free and resistant to random instabilities in the test environment.

Chapter 6, Testing the Behavior, will help you discover why testing the application in its current iteration becomes unmaintainable in the long run. Instead, we will start testing the desired behavior of the application, not the implementation.

Chapter 7, The Page Objects Pattern, covers one of the most undervalued and misunderstood topics when it comes to User Interface testing, that is, Page Objects. In this chapter, we will create a working Page Object testing framework and demonstrate how the tests can keep up with the new feature development cycle.

Chapter 8, Growing the Test Suite, will conclude this book with some basic tips on how to prioritize the growth of the test suite. Along the way, we will discuss how to keep our test stable and relevant to the whole team, no matter how often or big the changes are to the application being tested.

Appendix, Getting Started with Selenium, covers the initial setup of the user's computer. We will learn how to use the Command Line Interface terminal on Windows, Mac OSX, and Linux. We will install the Ruby programming language and Selenium WebDriver Ruby gem, followed by installation of the Firefox web browser. It concludes by explaining the test file and class nomenclature so that individuals new to the Ruby programming language can easily follow along with the tests.

What you need for this book

To get started with this book, you will need a basic understanding of what Selenium is, what it does, and basic programming skills. If you are able to create a simple `click` command in Selenium WebDriver and write a simple `loop` program in any programming language, you should be able to keep up with every example in this book. We will take the time to explain every line of code written in this book so that you are able to create the desired outcome in any situation you may find yourself in. There are some very small and simple software prerequisites that are needed. We will need to have access to the Command Line Interface terminal, Ruby runtime environment, and Firefox web browser. You can find the simple step-by-step setup instructions for all of these prerequisites in the *Appendix, Getting Started with Selenium.*

Who this book is for

This book is for anyone who wishes to write better automated tests. Whether you are writing your first Selenium test or have written hundreds of them, you will find this book useful to create a good test suite. However, this book is not only meant for writing better Selenium tests. A lot of the examples and techniques discussed in this book apply not only to Selenium WebDriver, but also to any automated tests written in any programming language.

Conventions

In this book, you will find a number of styles of text that distinguish between different kinds of information. Here are some examples of these styles, and an explanation of their meaning.

Code words in text, database table names, folder names, filenames, file extensions, pathnames, dummy URLs, user input, and Twitter handles are shown as follows: "You can even open the `search_test.html` file in your web browser and see how it looks!"

A block of code is set as follows:

```
more_info_buttons = special_items.collect do |special_item|
  special_item.find_element(:class, "more-info")
end
```

When we wish to draw your attention to a particular part of a code block, the relevant lines or items are set in bold:

```
require 'rubygems'
require 'selenium-webdriver'

selenium = Selenium::WebDriver.for(:firefox)
selenium.get("http://awful-valentine.com/")
selenium.find_element(:id, "searchinput").clear
selenium.find_element(:id, "searchinput").send_keys("cheese")
selenium.find_element(:id, "searchsubmit").click
selenium.quit
```

Any command-line input or output is written as follows:

```
ruby run_tests.rb
```

New terms and **important words** are shown in bold. Words that you see on the screen, in menus or dialog boxes for example, appear in the text like this: "Click on **Install Now** when it becomes clickable after several seconds."

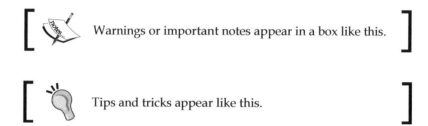

Warnings or important notes appear in a box like this.

Tips and tricks appear like this.

Reader feedback

Feedback from our readers is always welcome. Let us know what you think about this book—what you liked or may have disliked. Reader feedback is important for us to develop titles that you really get the most out of.

To send us general feedback, simply send an e-mail to feedback@packtpub.com, and mention the book title via the subject of your message.

If there is a topic that you have expertise in and you are interested in either writing or contributing to a book, see our author guide on www.packtpub.com/authors.

Customer support

Now that you are the proud owner of a Packt book, we have a number of things to help you to get the most from your purchase.

Downloading the example code

You can download the example code files for all Packt books you have purchased from your account at http://www.packtpub.com. If you purchased this book elsewhere, you can visit http://www.packtpub.com/support and register to have the files e-mailed directly to you.

Errata

Although we have taken every care to ensure the accuracy of our content, mistakes do happen. If you find a mistake in one of our books—maybe a mistake in the text or the code—we would be grateful if you would report this to us. By doing so, you can save other readers from frustration and help us improve subsequent versions of this book. If you find any errata, please report them by visiting http://www.packtpub. com/submit-errata, selecting your book, clicking on the **errata submission form** link, and entering the details of your errata. Once your errata are verified, your submission will be accepted and the errata will be uploaded on our website, or added to any list of existing errata, under the Errata section of that title. Any existing errata can be viewed by selecting your title from http://www.packtpub.com/support.

Piracy

Piracy of copyright material on the Internet is an ongoing problem across all media. At Packt, we take the protection of our copyright and licenses very seriously. If you come across any illegal copies of our works, in any form, on the Internet, please provide us with the location address or website name immediately so that we can pursue a remedy.

Please contact us at copyright@packtpub.com with a link to the suspected pirated material.

We appreciate your help in protecting our authors, and our ability to bring you valuable content.

Questions

You can contact us at questions@packtpub.com if you are having a problem with any aspect of the book, and we will do our best to address it.

1
Writing the First Test

"Self-education is, I firmly believe, the only kind of education there is."

-Isaac Asimov

In this book, we will simulate my personal experience of testing e-commerce systems. We will start by writing a very simple and crude test case, and we will refactor it and grow it into a *stable* and *reliable* test suite. A web store example might not apply to everyone's job, but the examples provided should be general enough to apply to any situation.

Today is our first day on the job; you and I are the sole members of the newly formed Quality Assurance team for the little start-up that sells Valentine's Day cards. It's a small company and the pay is not the greatest; however, just like any small start up, we get some company stock. This means that we can be very rich and famous if the website becomes popular. The website needs to stay operational and bug free, or our customers will never return and I will not be able to purchase that yacht I always wanted.

We know that we are short-staffed and need some automated tests to keep the quality high. However, first we need to convince the owner of the company that test automation is the right direction, instead of just testing everything by hand. We need to provide a cost-effective way to test the website and get quick results!

In this chapter, we will make an argument for using Selenium as our automation tool of choice and write a simple test to show how fast we can start building new tests. We will discuss the following topics along the way:

- Why you should use Selenium over other tools
- The Record and Playback pattern
- The Selenium IDE

- Recording a test with the Selenium IDE
- Selenium WebDriver
- Writing a test with Ruby
- The Test::Unit testing framework
- Interactive test debugging

Choosing Selenium over other tools

There are several reasons to use Selenium over other test automation tools out there:

- It is the right tool for the right job
- It is free of cost
- It is open source
- It is highly flexible

Right tool for the right job

Selenium is a great tool for testing web applications and interacting with the application like a real user would. It uses a real browser to click, type, and fill out forms. It is as close to a human user as you can get. It's the perfect tool for testing the flow of the web application from start to finish.

Price

Nothing can beat the free price tag! While there are other commercial products that have more advanced features available for purchase, they tend to run into tens of thousands of dollars per license. Selenium is so cheap that you will be able to finish this book and build a whole test suite without spending another dollar.

 As old anti-proverb states: *there is no free lunch, but there is always more cheese in the mousetrap*. A free tool does not mean that the tests will write themselves for free; there will always be expenditure on someone's time. By following good practices, we will not be able to eliminate this cost but will try to reduce it as much as possible in the long run.

Open source

Selenium is **Open source software (OSS)**, but this means more than "it is free". As with other OSS, with Selenium, you don't just get the product but you get a whole community; you become part of the family. The majority of Selenium developers cannot wait to help someone who is in need, or to share some really great workaround for a difficult problem they ran into. This sure beats paying for expensive and underwhelming technical support you get with a commercial product.

Flexibility

Selenium is incredibly flexible; because it is Java-based, you can run it on most operating systems or browsers. You can even use it to test iOS and Android browsers. On top of that, you can run it in "headless mode" with an emulation browser, or set up a grid to increase your capacity, but we will cover more on these topics later in the book.

The Record and Playback pattern

Let's start with the very first test development pattern: the Record and Playback pattern. This is the starting point with majority of Selenium and other automated user interface testing tools. The idea behind this approach of test development is to allow the user to record their normal testing activities and play them back through the testing tool at a later date.

Advantages of the Record and Playback pattern

Having a tool record our interaction with the application has several advantages; chief among them is the speed at which we can grow our test suite. Let's take a look at individual advantages:

- **Fast test growth**: This is the biggest selling point in most commercial tools available. A user is able to record new individual tests as fast as he or she can click on links. A large test suite can be created in hours instead of weeks.

- **No previous experience**: It does not require any experience with programming language, just click on the record button and click around. Let the tool write the actual test code.

- **Element lookup**: It is incredibly easy and useful, and there is no need to look at the page source to find the button by hand. Just click on record, click on the desired button, and the element location is recorded in the test for you.

Disadvantages of the Record and Playback pattern

The commercial testing tools will give you a very large list of great features, which may sound too good to be true. In actuality, these features probably are too good to be true; every recording tool has these and many more disadvantages:

- **Bad locators**: These are a common problem with recording tools. Often a tool will record the absolute path to an element. If the desired button shifts left or right on the page, the playback of the test might fail even though the application works perfectly fine.

- **Inflexible tests**: These are the only output from recording tools. Since the playback is identical to the recording process, the final result is an identical copy of the recording. However, what if a test needs to register a new unique user for each run? To accommodate this task, it often takes more time than to write the test by hand in a programming language.

- **Hardcoded test data**: It is a big problem if your tests need to be flexible and use different data depending on the environment. We will discuss test data in *Chapter 4, Data-driven Testing*.

- **Poorly written tests**: Just like many **WYSWYG** tools available for writing code, the task of creating something is simple. However, the maintenance becomes incredibly difficult, as variable names and method names might be poorly named or strangely nested within each other.

 What You See (is) What You Get (WYSWYG) is a name for tools that allow users to quickly mock up an application interface. Using the final product of a WYSWYG tool in production is generally considered a bad idea and should be avoided.

- **Duplicate code**: It is one of the examples of poorly written tests. Most recording tools are not intelligent enough to detect duplicate steps and will not reuse existing code. See the *The DRY testing pattern* section in *Chapter 3, Refactoring Tests*.

Getting started with the Selenium IDE

Now, let's get our hands dirty! We will be playing with **Selenium Interactive Development Environment (Selenium IDE or simply IDE)** in this section. IDE is one of the greatest starting points for the Selenium project. It allows someone who has never programmed in his or her life to record a useful test in a matter of minutes and start adding new tests to the test suite in no time.

Installing the Selenium IDE

Selenium IDE is a browser plugin that only works in Firefox browser. It is easy to install and integrates well with the functionality of the browser. Use these easy-to-follow steps to install the IDE in the browser:

1. In your Firefox browser, navigate to the Selenium website at `http://seleniumhq.org`:

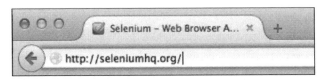

2. Click on the **Download Selenium** link on the home page shown:

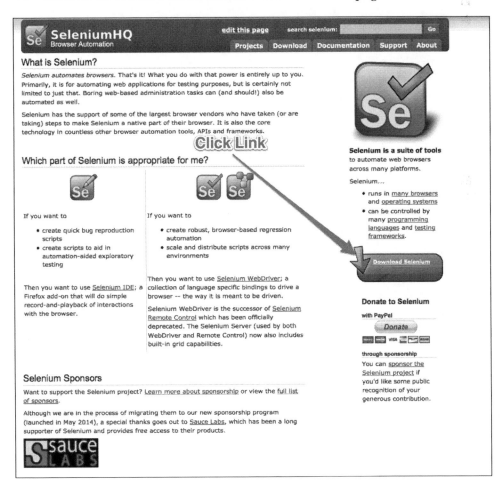

3. In the **Selenium IDE** section on the **Download** page, click on the link for the latest released version, as shown here:

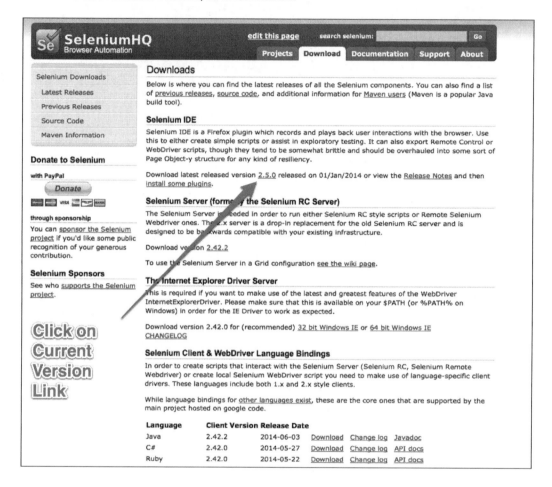

4. Allow Selenium to be installed on your computer by clicking on **Allow** on the following permission dialog:

5. The following dialog will show you all of the Selenium IDE components that will be installed on your browser. Click on **Install Now** when it becomes clickable after several seconds. The installation dialog is shown in the following screenshot:

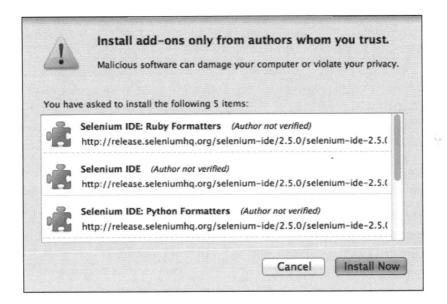

6. Restart Firefox.

   Now that the plugins have been installed, you should see a little icon in the browser:

7. Clicking on that button will reveal the Selenium IDE window, as shown in the following screenshot:

We are now ready to go!

Recording our first test

Just like many commercial testing tools, the Selenium IDE supports the Record-Playback style of writing tests. The IDE monitors your browser and notes down any actions that you perform. By compiling a list of actions, a test slowly emerges. Let's start recording our first test by following these steps:

1. Open the Selenium IDE in the Firefox browser and make sure the recording mode is on, as shown in following screenshot:

Note that the recording indicator is a little difficult to read since it does not change color when on or off. The main difference is a slightly light gray square around the button when it's on. This is one of several major drawbacks of Selenium IDE.

2. In a new tab, navigate to `http://awful-valentine.com`, as shown in the following screenshot:

3. Click on the search text field and type in cheese in the search bar and click on the submit button. The following screenshot shows the search box and the submit button:

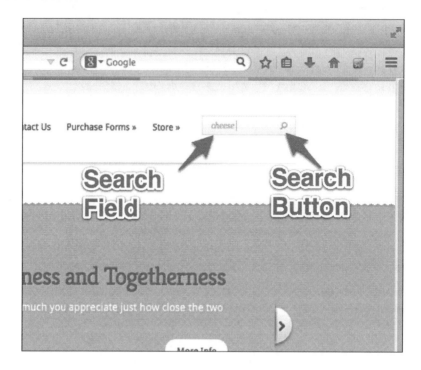

As we are performing these actions, the IDE is recording all of them in the background. We can inspect all of the recorded actions in the IDE window, as shown in the following screenshot:

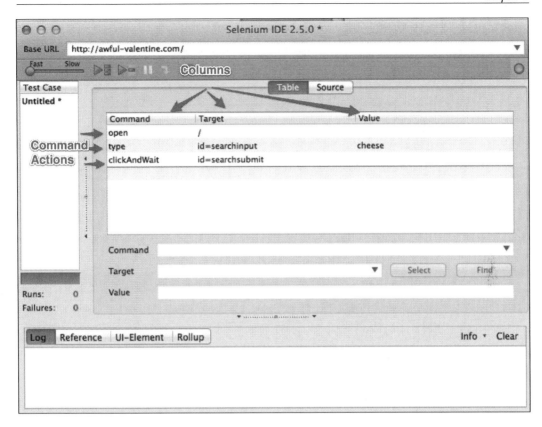

Let's walk through the table inside the IDE window to get a better understanding of each item.

The table has three columns in it:

- The first column is **Command**. This is where the action of the command is defined, such as a click or type.
- The second column is **Target**, where the command will be performed.
- Finally, the third column is **Value**. This section is only used when the target element, such as a text field, needs some text inserted into it.

We have our simple script now; let's save it so we can reuse it later.

Saving the test

Our next step is to save the test run to a file:

1. Click on the **File** option:

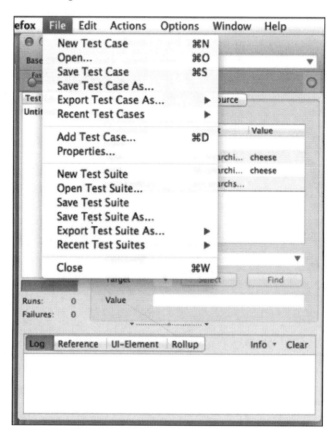

2. Choose **Save Test Case**.

3. Name the file `search_test.html` and save it.

Notice that we saved the test as an HTML file. This is because Selenese, the language that the IDE uses to record and playback tests, is just an HTML table. You can even open the `search_test.html` file in your web browser and see how it looks! In the following screenshot, we have Selenium IDE and the saved test opens side by side for easy comparison:

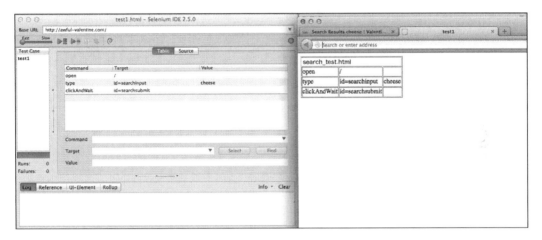

Right away, you can see that the IDE (on the left) and the saved Selenese output displayed in a web browser (on the right) look extremely similar.

Understanding Selenium commands

In this section, we will walk through the saved test from the IDE, which is written in a language called Selenese. We will then compare the Selenese commands to the commands written in a real programming language.

> The code and the step-by-step instructions on how to test it on Windows and other operating systems can be found at `https://github.com/dimacus/SeleniumBestPracticesBook`.

Reading Selenese

If you ever see the HTML source code of any web page, Selenese will not be a new concept for you. Selenese can simply be described as an HTML table with a table row as a test command. Let's take a closer look at it. Open the `search_test.html` file in your editor of choice. The whole test should look like this:

```
1   <?xml version="1.0" encoding="UTF-8"?>
2   <!DOCTYPE html PUBLIC "-//W3C//DTD XHTML 1.0 Strict//EN" "http://www.w
3   <html xmlns="http://www.w3.org/1999/xhtml" xml:lang="en" lang="en">
4   <head profile="http://selenium-ide.openqa.org/profiles/test-case">
5   <meta http-equiv="Content-Type" content="text/html; charset=UTF-8" />
6   <link rel="selenium.base" href="http://awful-valentine.com/" />
7   <title>search_test</title>
8   </head>
9   <body>
10  <table cellpadding="1" cellspacing="1" border="1">
11  <thead>
12  <tr><td rowspan="1" colspan="3">test1</td></tr>
13  </thead><tbody>
14  <tr>
15      <td>open</td>
16      <td>/</td>
17      <td></td>
18  </tr>
19  <tr>
20      <td>type</td>
21      <td>id=searchinput</td>
22      <td>cheese</td>
23  </tr>
24  <tr>
25      <td>clickAndWait</td>
26      <td>id=searchsubmit</td>
27      <td></td>
28  </tr>
29
30  </tbody></table>
31  </body>
32  </html>
33
```

We will ignore the first five lines of the code, as it has no practical application for us at this point. On line **6**, you will find the following code:

```
6   <link rel="selenium.base" href="http://awful-valentine.com/" />
```

The preceding line declares the base domain URL for our tests.

 One of the biggest weaknesses in Selenium 1 (RC) is that it was written in JavaScript, which exposes security issues with third-party domains running arbitrary JavaScript code on any website. The security experts implemented strict rules to prevent **Cross-Site Scripting (XSS)**. Thus, Selenium IDE and RC will not be able to test multiple websites in a single test run.

Our next section of interest is the code on lines **14** to **18**, where a single **table row (tr)** contains our first command in three **table data (td)** sections. Test lines 14 to 18 are shown here:

```
14   <tr>
15       <td>open</td>
16       <td>/</td>
17       <td></td>
18   </tr>
```

The first TD matches the **Command** column in the IDE, and in this case the command is to open a given URL.

The second TD matches the **Target** column in the IDE and is telling the test to open the root of the base URL from line 6.

 You can tweak your test here by adding a direct link to a page you want, such as /index.html or /register. This will allow you to go directly to the page you wish to test.

Comparing Ruby to Selenese

Let's look at the commands we just learned in the IDE and Selenese and how they translate into the Ruby language. In the case of Ruby, we will only look at the key commands and how they translate from Selenese into Ruby. The goal of this exercise is to take away some of the intimidation factor of moving to a programming language for someone who may never have seen software code before.

To start, let's look back at the HTML table that is the Selenese output:

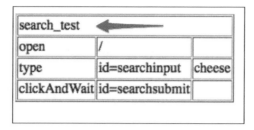

The first line in this table is the name of the test, which happens to be `search_test`.

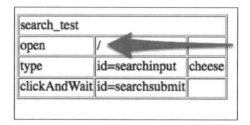

The second item, shown in the preceding screenshot is the open command to the root (/) of the base domain URL. So, the browser will navigate to this exact address `http://awful-valentine.com/`.

Downloading the example code

You can download the example code files for all Packt books you have purchased from your account at `http://www.packtpub.com`. If you purchased this book elsewhere, you can visit `http://www.packtpub.com/support` and register to have the files e-mailed directly to you.

In Ruby, the `open` command translates into a very straightforward `get` method call. The code looks like this:

```
selenium.get("http://awful-valentine.com/")
```

Note that we didn't have to use base URL like we did with Selenese. WebDriver talks directly to the web browser, not through JavaScript; this eliminates XSS limitations, and you can test as many websites as you want in a single test run.

Once the browser navigates to the website we want, it needs to locate the search field and input the search term. In the `search_test` table, it is in the third line:

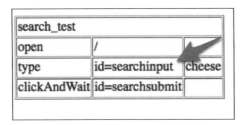

search_test		
open	/	
type	id=searchinput	cheese
clickAndWait	id=searchsubmit	

Since this is a complex multistep action, let's break it down into smaller chunks:

1. Find the text field element with the help of the `find_element` method by passing it the HTML ID of the text field (`searchInput`), and then store the element in the element variable:

   ```
   element = selenium.find_element(:id, "searchInput")
   ```

2. Once the text field is located and stored in the `element` variable, we will type the `cheese` string into it by using the `send_keys` method:

   ```
   element.send_keys("cheese")
   ```

3. We have now typed the text we wanted into the search bar. We used the `element` variable to store the reference to the text field, and then applied some typing action on that variable.

4. We can use **method chaining** to get the same result in a more condensed version; the search and type text action would look like the following code with method chaining:

   ```
   selenium.find_element(:id, "searchInput").send_keys("cheese")
   ```

Method chaining is a common type of syntax that allows the programmer to invoke multiple method calls without using intermittent variables. Each method call in the chain returns an object that answers to the next method call in the chain. We will go deeper into object-oriented programming in the *The Page Objects pattern* section of *Chapter 7, The Page Objects Pattern*.

The last action our test performs is clicking on the search submit button. In the Selenese table, it is the fourth row of our test:

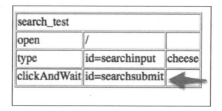

search_test		
open	/	
type	id=searchinput	cheese
clickAndWait	id=searchsubmit	

5. Using method chaining as before, we will find the submit button and send a `click` command to it:

```
selenium.find_element(:id, "searchsubmit").click
```

The `clickAndWait` command translates to a simple `click` method call in Ruby.

> Notice that with Selenium WebDriver, the *wait for page to load* part of the `clickAndWait` command is implicit. As of Selenium 2, when navigating from page to page, Selenium will automatically wait for the new page to finish loading. This, however, does not apply for any AJAX requests to finish. We will discuss AJAX waits in *Chapter 5, Stabilizing the Tests*.

Comparing Selenium commands in multiple languages

Translating recorded tests from IDE into Ruby is rather simple, and we can get started even if we do not have any previous programming experience; learning as we go works just fine. The most exciting part is that these commands are even easier to translate from Ruby to any other programming language. Here are a couple of examples of the usage of the `sendKeys()` method that we used in the preceding example:

Language	Command
Ruby	`element.send_keys("cheese");`
Java	`element.sendKeys("cheese");`
C-Sharp	`element.SendKeys("cheese");`
Python	`element.send_keys("cheese");`
JavaScript	`element.sendKeys("cheese");`

The consistency of the WebDriver API makes it incredibly easy to port your knowledge of the test from one language to another. This is great news for you, the test engineer, because you become more valuable to your company. You can be dropped in on any web project, written in any programming language, and start writing tests right away! Information and examples of different WebDriver commands in any programming language can be found at http://docs.seleniumhq.org/docs/.

The preceding example is slightly oversimplified. The action commands are written in the same format from programming language to programming language. However, writing code in different kinds of languages, such as compiled VS interpreted, will have their own idioms and best practices. Some actions that work well in Ruby would be wasteful and counterintuitive in Java.

Writing a Selenium test in Ruby

In this section, we will implement our test case completely in Ruby. Writing a test in a new language can be intimidating, but don't despair because we will walk through and talk about every command we use. This book will not make you a great Ruby developer, but it will get you comfortable enough to write tests on your own!

 At this point, it is assumed that you already have Ruby and the selenium-webdriver gem installed on your computer. Please refer to *Appendix, Getting Started with Selenium,* for step-by-step installation instructions.

Our fully ported test into Ruby looks like this:

```ruby
require 'rubygems'
require 'selenium-webdriver'

selenium = Selenium::WebDriver.for(:firefox)
selenium.get("http://awful-valentine.com/")
selenium.find_element(:id, "searchinput").clear
selenium.find_element(:id, "searchinput").send_keys("cheese")
selenium.find_element(:id, "searchsubmit").click
selenium.quit
```

As you can see, there are only a couple of new lines that we didn't see before. The first two lines are require 'rubygems' and require 'selenium-webdriver', which tell the Ruby interpreter that we want to use some gems; specifically, we want to the selenium-webdriver gem:

```ruby
selenium = Selenium::WebDriver.for(:firefox)
```

In the preceding line, we request a new instance of the Firefox browser, and store it in the `selenium` variable. From this point on, we will reference back the `selenium` variable anytime we wish to give new directions to Firefox browsers. The code is as follows:

```
selenium.find_element(:id, "searchinput").clear
```

The preceding line clears any previous text from the search field. This is just a good practice anytime you wish to fill out any text field, because you never know what was left over there after some other test.

> When writing a Selenium test, it is always a good practice to send a `clear` command into every text field you wish to fill out. Due to the unpredictable nature of JavaScript from browser to browser, the default text might not be cleared before the new desired text is entered by Selenium. By explicitly clearing each field, we avoid test instabilities.

Finally, `selenium.quit` is the final command of our test, which closes the Firefox browser and stops any WebDriver processes we started at the beginning of our test.

Save our test to a file as `search_test.rb`, and then run the following command in the terminal:

```
ruby search_test.rb
```

> The preceding command assumes that `search_test.rb` is located in the current directory that your terminal is located in. You may need to look up some basic command-line navigation to find the location of your `search_test.rb` file.

After you run this command, you will see a Firefox window open; navigate to your website and search for `cheese`. Congratulations! Our test has been ported from Selenium IDE to Ruby, and we learned some new, fun skills such as simple Ruby commands and command-line navigation in the process!

Introducing Test::Unit

Now that we have ported our test into Ruby, you probably noticed that even though our test does some stuff, it actually does not really test anything. Yes, it searches for `cheese` on the website, but it does not actually validate that anything was found or not found. As far as we are concerned, this test is a complete failure, because it not only *doesn't test anything* useful, but also because it has *no failure* condition—it will always pass.

We could write some checks in our current script to check that the search page returns the results we care about. However, this is a pretty good time to introduce `Test::Unit`. The `Test::Unit` framework is a simple testing framework that comes with Ruby. Testing frameworks allows us to better organize our individual tests and verify that everything on the page looks as expected with built-in methods called assertions.

> An assertion is what a test framework uses to confirm that something is a certain way. Assertions need two things to work—an expected outcome and an actual outcome. The expected outcome is defined in the test and the actual outcome is the result from the application when we run the test.

Let's convert our search test to use the `Test::Unit` framework. We will do this in three steps:

1. Convert the test file into a `CheeseFinderTest` class that inherits functionality from the `Test::Unit` framework.

2. Save the new test as `cheese_finder_test.rb`.

> Even though it is not required, Ruby convention demands us to save the file name to match the name of the class contained in the file.

3. Add an assertion to make the test meaningful.

After completing the first step, our test file will look like this:

```ruby
1  require 'rubygems'
2  require 'selenium-webdriver'
3  require 'test/unit'
4
5  class CheeseFinderTests < Test::Unit::TestCase
6
7    def test_find_some_cheese
8      selenium = Selenium::WebDriver.for(:firefox)
9      selenium.get("http://awful-valentine.com/")
10     selenium.find_element(:id, "searchinput").clear
11     selenium.find_element(:id, "searchinput").send_keys("cheese")
12     selenium.find_element(:id, "searchsubmit").click
13
14     selenium.quit
15    end
16
17  end
```

As you can see, only a couple of lines in our test case actually changed:

- For starters, we pulled in a new `require 'test/unit'` gem on line 3
- Next, we declared a new class on line 5 to be `CheeseFinderTests`
- Finally, we created a new method called `test_find_some_cheese` that has all of our test code

 In the `Test::Unit` framework, all of the test method names have to start with `test_` or they will be ignored.

- Let's save this to `cheese_finder_test.rb` and run the following command in the terminal:

```
ruby cheese_finder_test.rb
```

The following screenshot shows the output of the test run. The period (.) character in the middle of output, pointed out by the arrow, represents a single passing test. If a given test fails, you will see an `F` character in that position:

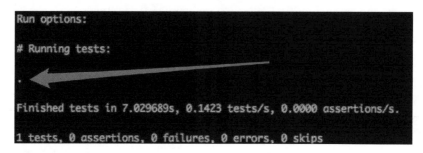

This is pretty cool, isn't it? We got all of this information about our test by only adding 3 new lines of actual code! As our suite keeps growing, these statistics will continue to change, and the test count should keep going up while failure count should stay down.

However, as we can still see, there are 0 assertions in our test. Let's add some assertions so that we are actually testing something!

Introducing asserts

`Test::Unit` comes with many different assertions, and the most commonly used ones are `assert` and `assert_equal` to test whether something is true or two items equal each other, respectively. In this test case, we will be using the `assert` method to check whether the search for `cheese` gives the **No Results Found** message.

A list of all supported assertions can be found at `http://ruby-doc.org/stdlib-2.1.0/libdoc/test/unit/rdoc/Test/Unit/Assertions.html`.

Let's walk through the individual steps required to add assertions to our tests:

1. To make this assertion work, we will use the `find_element` method we used previously to find the `entry` class on the page; the `entry` DIV will contain all of the search results on the page. The code for this is as follows:

   ```
   selenium.find_element(:class, "entry")
   ```

2. Once we find the `entry` element, we can use the `text` method to get the full string seen on the page:

   ```
   selenium.find_element(:class, "entry").text
   ```

3. Finally, we will use the `include?` method on the returned text string. This Ruby method returns `true` if the characters we are looking for are present in the string. The code looks something like this:

   ```
   selenium.find_element(:class, "entry").text.include?("No Results Found")
   ```

4. After all of this is set up for the assertion, we can now pass in the result of the word search into an assertion. As long as we keep getting **No Results Found**, our tests will keep passing. Let's take a look at the final version of our test:

```ruby
1   require 'rubygems'
2   require 'selenium-webdriver'
3   require 'test/unit'
4
5   class CheeseFinderTests < Test::Unit::TestCase
6
7     def test_find_some_cheese
8       selenium = Selenium::WebDriver.for(:firefox)
9       selenium.get("http://awful-valentine.com/")
10      selenium.find_element(:id, "searchinput").clear
11      selenium.find_element(:id, "searchinput").send_keys("cheese")
12      selenium.find_element(:id, "searchsubmit").click
13      assert(selenium.find_element(:class, "entry").text.include?("No Results Found"))
14      selenium.quit
15    end
16
17  end
```

Let's rerun our test; we should now see (as shown in the following screenshot) that the assertion count went up from 0 to 1:

```
Run options:

# Running tests:

.

Finished tests in 7.437526s, 0.1345 tests/s, 0.1345 assertions/s.

1 tests, 1 assertions, 0 failures, 0 errors, 0 skips
```

Our test is now officially testing the website! But we are not done yet; let's see what will happen when we force it to fail. Let's modify line 13 to expect a different result:

 Never consider a test complete unless you have seen it fail due to incorrect expectations. Often in a rush to get a test complete, we forget to test that it fails when it should, which gives us false green builds. These types of tests are not just useless, but harmful as they give us a false sense of security about the build.

Our modified code looks like the following:

```
13    assert(selenium.find_element(:class, "entry").text.include?("5 Results Found"))
```

By modifying the expected result to say **5 Results Found**, our test will fail in the following manner:

```
Run options:

# Running tests:

F

Finished tests in 6.664776s, 0.1500 tests/s, 0.1500 assertions/s.

  1) Failure:
test_find_some_cheese(CheeseFinderTests) [cheese_finder_test.rb:13]:
Failed assertion, no message given.

1 tests, 1 assertions, 1 failures, 0 errors, 0 skips
```

Our test has passed once and failed once, we can officially call it complete!

> In the current state of our test, on assertion failure the test suite exits but does not close the Firefox window. This allows us to examine the last page our test finished on. In *Chapter 3, Refactoring Tests*, we will discuss the teardown method, which will clean up the test environment every time the test finishes.

Interactive test debugging

Nothing is more exciting than to see your tests running, and running fast—really fast! Computers are great at taking bad instructions and running them really fast. The problem, of course, comes from the fact that when something goes wrong it is too fast for you to see it. You will run into a test failure, which no one can explain, almost on a daily basis. Tests, which fail intermittently, can be the source of frustration in your life. But don't despair; there are ways to track them down and fix them.

We will go into detail on how to track down and get rid of intermittent test failures in *Chapter 5, Stabilizing the Tests*. But in this section, we will take a look at a simple tool built into Ruby, called debug. Since Ruby is an interpreted language, you are able to stop test execution on any of your test environments without any fancy debugging tools. Let's play around with it, I promise it will be fun! Perform the following steps:

1. Let's add one simple line, require 'debug', to the beginning of our test so that it looks like this:

```
7   def test_find_some_cheese
8     selenium = Selenium::WebDriver.for(:firefox)
9     require 'debug'
10    selenium.get("http://awful-valentine.com/")
```

2. Now save it and run the test again. You will see that a Firefox window opened up and is just sitting on a blank white page. Take a look at the terminal; it will look something like this:

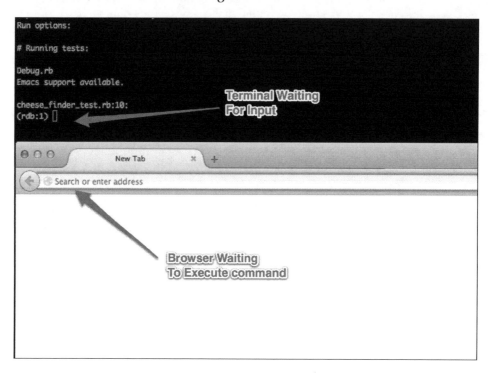

We have halted our test execution and entered into the **Interactive Ruby Shell (irb)**, which is a command-line tool for controlling Ruby. This is a great tool for debugging tests, because all of the memory objects are available at your fingertips. You can "quite literally" control your tests from here if you type in the proper commands. Let's take it for a spin.

In the terminal irb session, type in `selenium.get("http://seleniumhq.org")` and hit the *return* (*Enter*) key on the keyboard.

> With Ruby 2.X, you will need to press the *n* + *return* buttons before you are able to take advantage of the `selenium` variable. Ruby 2.X tends to halt the execution in the `Kernel` class, which is one step before line 10 of our test file. By sending the next line command in irb, we step back into the test file and have access to the `selenium` variable.

Now watch the browser navigate to Selenium's website! You can run clicks, asserts, or anything else your tests can do and more. You are able to walk through your tests one line at the time, step into any method, or completely alter the course of the test. Here are some basic commands on how to control your test:

Description	Command
Next line in the test	n
Step into method	s
Continue	c
Exit irb and continue execution	exit

The debugging tool mentioned here is by far the simplest tool available. It is built into every version of Ruby, but will not give us any fancy features. In compiled languages such as Java or C#, we can rely on the IDE to provide a user interface rich debugger. For a feature-rich debugger in Ruby, check out the Pry gem found at http://pryrepl.org/.

Using the debugger tool can be a little intimidating at times. If you ever get stuck, just close the terminal window and start again. You will soon be as comfortable with the debugger as with any other tool in your arsenal.

Summary

This concludes our first chapter; we got a lot accomplished in it. First we discussed the advantages of using Selenium and other OSS tools over the expensive commercial tools. After that we installed Selenium IDE and recorded our first test script, followed by the step-by-step deconstruction of each command performed in the script.

We then proceeded to convert the recorded test into Ruby programming language, comparing each command from the IDE with its Ruby equivalent. Finally, we started working with the Test::Unit testing framework and then learned about test assertions. We finished the chapter by making the test fail on purpose and played with the Ruby debugger. In the next chapter, we will add a couple of new tests and start to dive deeper into the Test::Unit framework. We will also talk about test suite design patterns that emerge from growing your test suite.

2
The Spaghetti Pattern

"Always code as if the guy who ends up maintaining your code will be a violent psychopath who knows where you live."

-Martin Golding

Writing and maintaining any form of software is like fighting entropy; given enough time and changes, any code base will gradually decline into disorder. A test suite is a closed system; if you do not provide energy in constant upkeep and planning, the suite will deteriorate and will fail constantly. Every new feature and line of code added to our website makes our test suite obsolete. The only way to fight back these natural forces is to constantly upgrade and improve existing tests.

In this chapter, we will start to grow our test suite organically and take a look at an anti-pattern called the **Spaghetti pattern**. Along the way, we will pick up some more basic skills, such as using **XPath** and **CSS selectors** to locate the elements on a web page.

 The term *anti-pattern* was inspired by a great book on software design called *Design Patterns: Elements of Reusable Object-Oriented Software* by Erich Gamma, Richard Helm, Ralph Johnson, and John Vlissides, published by *Addison-Wesley Professional* and is roughly defined as a common practice, which seems appropriate for current situation, but has a lot of unintended side effects. Furthermore, a better solution for the problem does exist, but is typically ignored in favor of the initial obvious but wrong solution.

In order to write the new tests in this chapter, we will cover the following topics:

- Spaghetti pattern
- Element locator strategies
- XPath and CSS selector query languages

- Relative and absolute path
- Browser inspector tool
- Test run order
- Chain Linked pattern
- Big Ball of Mud pattern

Introducing the Spaghetti pattern

In automated test projects, the Spaghetti pattern development is characterized by lack of perceived architecture and design. This style of test development evokes an image of bowl of spaghetti, where each strand of spaghetti can represent a single test or multiple tests intertwined so tightly together that it becomes difficult to tell one apart from another. Furthermore, it is close to impossible to understand anything at a glance without spending time fishing out and untangling each individual strand of spaghetti from the bowl.

Tests in this pattern not only depend on the execution order of all the tests, but also tend to over-share internal private components with each other. The run order is important because each test is not self sufficient and independent, and thus needs previously run tests to set up the test environment. For example, a login test requires the registration test to successfully register a new user, instead of having an existing user or registering one on its own. Furthermore, variables in the test suite are shared on a global level, allowing individual tests too much control over the whole test suite.

 The Spaghetti pattern is a close relative to the Chain Linked pattern and the Big Ball of Mud pattern. We will discuss both of these patterns at the end of this chapter.

Advantages of the Spaghetti pattern

Even though the Spaghetti pattern is an anti-pattern, it is not without some positive elements. Let's take a look at several positives:

- **Quick start**: The reason that this type of a development pattern is initially popular is because it is by far the easiest and fastest way to get going. No need to sit down and plan ahead; just use Record and Playback to record one long test session and split it up into smaller chunks.

- **Smaller code base**: Since all the tests depend on each other, we do not need to repeat test actions within individual tests. As a result, each individual test is smaller in code size, and we do not need to have unique test data for each test.

This is by far the worst justification for any anti-pattern. We no longer live in the Commodore 64 days; if a test or a piece of code needs an additional 20 lines of code to become easy to comprehend, then always choose verbosity over brevity.

- **Smoke tests**: By definition, smoke tests need to be fast, brief, and leave as small a test data footprint as possible. Having several tests that reuse a single registered user in production is a good practice. No need to fill up the production database with test users.

We will discuss different test suite types, including smoke tests, in more detail in *Chapter 8, Growing the Test Suite*.

Disadvantages of the Spaghetti pattern

Aside from the ability to get going fast, the Spaghetti pattern has many disadvantages:

- **Anti-pattern**: Building one test on top of another seems like a great idea at first. After all, this is how we test applications when we do it manually. However, in context of test automation, this leads to long-term maintainability problems. Thus, it is considered an anti-pattern.
- **Tight coupling**: The more tightly integrated individual parts of the application are, the more indistinguishable they are from each other. Tight coupling prevents code reusability and leads to duplication.

We will concentrate on code reusability and decoupling in *Chapter 3, Refactoring Tests*.

No random order: Dependence on the strict order of execution leads to the inability to run our tests in a random order. This might not seem like a problem at first, until we need to debug test data pollution in the test suite.

> Data pollution occurs when a certain test puts the test environment into an unrecoverable state by adding unexpected data into the database or memory. If that test is executed last in the test suite, an application crash might not be detected until the execution order is accidentally switched.

- **No parallel test runs**: Once the test suite grows in size, we might wish to reduce the total execution time by running multiple tests in parallel. Having each test depend on the execution order of the whole suite will prevent us from accomplishing this task.

- **Covers up failures**: A failure in the beginning of the test suite can prevent the execution of the entire test suite. Several tests that would have failed later in the suite are never executed.

- **No resilience**: Certain tests are not able to fulfill their target goals. A credit card processing test that does not know how to register a required user will never run if the user registration test fails due to an unrelated issue.

Testing the product review functionality

Our website, like many other modern websites, allows users to leave positive and negative feedback on a given product. Higher-rated comments on any given product can provide a much needed boost in sales. As with any situation involving monetary incentives, someone will try to game the system and make money in the process. So, aside from the ability to leave a comment, our website has a rudimentary fraud prevention system. It will prevent any suspiciously duplicate comments/ratings from being added to any product.

It is now our task to test both of these features. So, let's explicitly state the target goals of the tests we will now implement:

- As a website user, I should be able to leave a product review for any product, and the resulting review should be immediately visible on the product's page
- As a fraudulent user, I should be prevented from posting duplicate product reviews on our website

Starting a product review test

Let's start off by making a new file, `product_review_test.rb`. In this file, we will be writing our tests for this chapter. We will copy and paste most of the initial boilerplate from `cheese_finder_test.rb` from the previous chapter.

 Boilerplate code refers to parts of the code that remain close to identical between different files/classes. Several examples of boilerplate are `includes`, `requires`, and `imports`. These are used by most programming languages to specify dependencies used in the current file.

The starting point of our test will look like this:

```ruby
1   require 'rubygems'
2   require 'selenium-webdriver'          ◄── Boilerplate
3   require 'test/unit'
                          Test class name
4
5   class ProductReview < Test::Unit::TestCase
6     def test_add_new_review              ◄── New test name
7       selenium = Selenium::WebDriver.for(:firefox)
8       selenium.get("http://awful-valentine.com/")
9
10      #Test work goes here
11
12      selenium.quit
13    end
14  end
```

As described in the previous chapter, in our test we created an instance of `selenium` and sent it a command to navigate to our website of choice. Later, we have a comment `#Test work goes here` followed by a command to close the instance of Firefox we are using with `selenium.quit`.

 The test name and class name for this file has changed. You can find a more detailed explanation of Ruby class names under the *Understanding test class naming* section, in *Appendix, Getting Started with Selenium*.

The steps of our new product review test are listed as follows:

1. Locate and click on the **MORE INFO** button for the product of your choice.

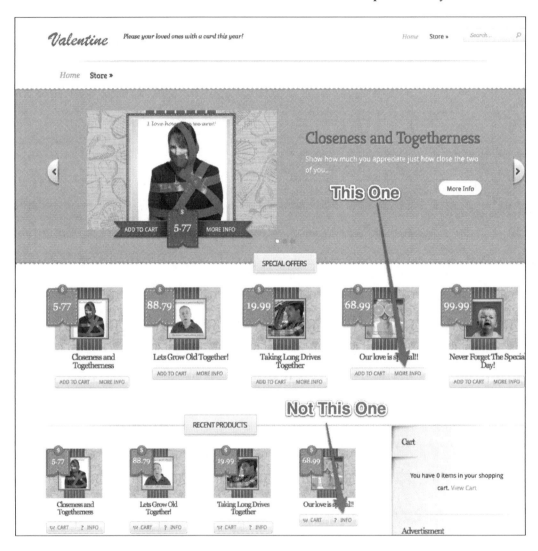

2. Check whether the correct product was selected.

3. Fill in the user information, comment, and rating and submit the review.

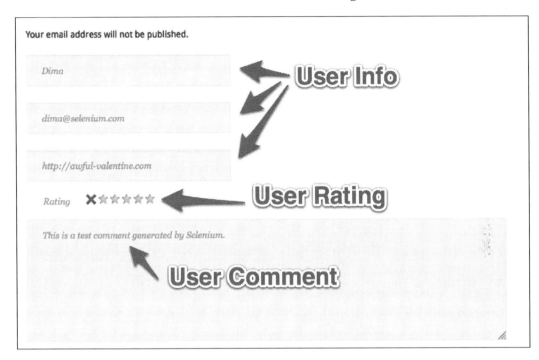

4. Check whether the product review is properly saved:

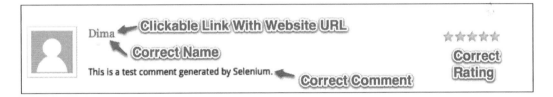

Let's implement our test!

Locating elements on the page

The first step of the `test_add_new_review` implementation is to navigate to the home page of our site and click on the **MORE INFO** button of the product we wish to review. However, it has to be the product in the **SPECIAL OFFERS** section, as shown in the following screenshot:

Since there are multiple products with the **MORE INFO** button and sometimes we have the same product on the page multiple times, each with the **MORE INFO** button, the task seems impossibly hard. The following screenshot shows an example of a product with three occurrences of the **MORE INFO** button:

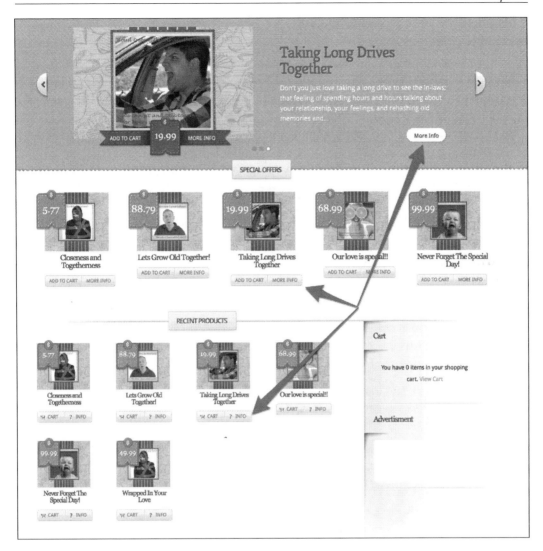

But fret not; the solution is extremely simple once we learn about different ways of locating elements on the page. The first step is to locate the element we want to interact with on the page. For this purpose, most modern browsers have a built-in page inspector.

Using a browser's element inspector

Until recently, when writing an automated test, we would have to open up the HTML source of any given page and hunt through the code to find the element we want. Needless to say, this was difficult and time-consuming. In recent iterations of Firefox and Chrome browsers, the functionality of the Firebug plugin was copied into the browser, allowing users to interactively inspect any element on the page. This makes our life as test automators a lot easier! Let's get our hands dirty with the page inspector.

 Firebug was one of the earliest Firefox plugins, which gave users the ability to inspect the elements on the page, directly interact with CSS, and do much more. The majority of built-in inspectors function identically to Firebug. This plugin is still backwards compatible with Firefox Version 3, and it is a great option for users who are not able to use latest version of Firefox or Chrome. For more info, visit `https://addons.mozilla.org/en-US/firefox/addon/firebug/`.

To inspect the desired element, all we have to do is right click on the **MORE INFO** button of the product and select the **Inspect Element** option from the context menu, as shown in the following screenshot:

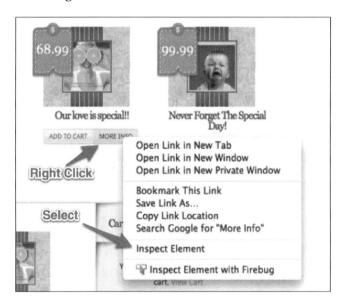

Once the inspector window opens, we will see the following breakdown of the page source:

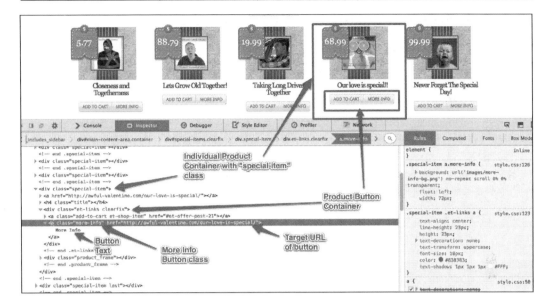

If you ever feel lost looking at the inspector, just remember, hovering over a piece of HTML code will highlight that element on the page.

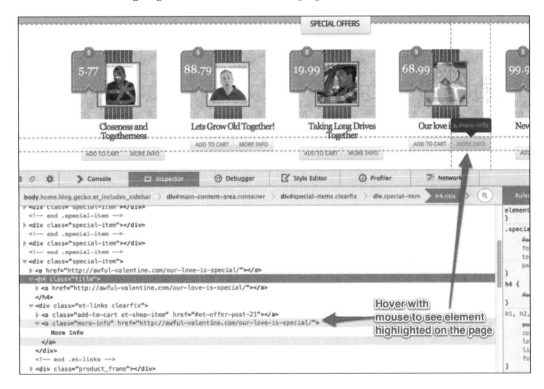

Using the element IDs, tags, classes, and position within parent elements, we are able to express an exact location of any element on the page. Let's talk about different ways of expressing the element locations next.

Introducing locator strategies

When giving driving direction to someone, we can express said instructions in multiple ways. We can show the destination on a map or give a turn-by-turn instruction, or even give the individual the final address and let them use a GPS to find the address. Similarly, WebDriver allows us to find an element through the following strategies:

- **ID**: This finds an element that has an ID provided. By far, it's the best way to locate any element because we can jump directly to the element without having to deal with surrounding elements or parent elements.

> Even though finding an element by ID is the best location strategy, we have to use it with care. There is no guarantee that an element we want will have an ID attached to it, or that a given element ID is unique.

- **Class name**: This will locate an element(s) with a given class name.

> We might get different search results if we use the `find_element` method vs `find_elements`. The first method will return the first element found out of all matches on the page; the second method will return all matching elements. In our case, searching for all of the buttons with a class of more information will return many results. Thus, it is not the most useful approach.

- **Link text**: This finds a link that has an exact text in it; in our case, **MORE INFO**.

> Since most modern website use links that are styled with CSS to look like buttons, the term link and button are used interchangeably in this book.

- **Partial link text**: This is similar to link text locator, but allows a wild card search for partial text match. In our case a search for info will return all of the **MORE INFO** buttons.
- **Name**: This searches for all elements that have a name property.

 The name is not the most popular element property in modern websites, thus this locator strategy is rarely used.

- **Tag name**: This searches for an element's tag name, such as input or label.
- **CSS selector**: This searches for elements with custom-written CSS selector style query.
- **XPath**: This searches for elements with custom-written XPath style query.

In a perfect world, all of the buttons on the home page would have unique IDs. Within the ID, we would be able to specify the product name or SKU number and the location of the product, such as the **Special Offers** section or in the **Featured** section. In that case, if we ever wanted to click on the exact **MORE INFO** button we want, all that we would have to do is write this one line:

```
selenium.find_element(:id, "more-info-product-25-special-offer").click
```

Sadly, things are typically not this simple, and elements don't have unique IDs that we can use. More often than not, we have to find the location of the element using CSS selectors or XPath; in the next section, we will learn about these advanced techniques.

 Just because our website does not have unique IDs, it does not mean we have to give up and try to find a difficult solution for finding and element. It is amazing how often a unique identifier can be added to the website by simply talking to the developers and making a good case for it. If an argument such as "it will make testing much simpler for me" does not work, an argument of making the website accessible for the blind might work. Screen readers work best with lots of uniquely identifiable elements.

Using advanced locator strategies

Searching for an element by using the unique ID of the element is similar to giving your friends the address of the party and letting them figure out the directions with a smart phone. Aside from several glitches in the navigation software, it is the fastest and simplest way to get around. However, when a smart phone or a map is not available, we have to write directions on a napkin.

We can give directions in two ways, the absolute path and relative path. Let's compare these two types of directions:

- **Absolute path**: This is a very detailed set of instructions starting from the friend's house and gives every turn, road name, number, and even the distance between each turn. My dad typically gives directions in this manner.

- **Relative path**: This approach is a little more relaxed and is the preferred way of giving directions by my mother. These directions typically look like this: "Get to that big store where we bought this rug from, you remember? Then take a left and drive until you see the blue gas station, turn around, and turn right on the second stop sign you see."

Both approaches have their own advantages and disadvantages. The absolute path requires the least amount of thinking and is simplest to follow. However, it is very rigid and becomes useless if there is a traffic accident on the way and we need to find new directions. The relative path requires the most concentration from the driver, but at the same time is the most flexible. By setting the starting point of the directions at a known location that is close to the destination, it allows the driver to take any route he or she wishes.

As you already guessed, the driving directions example is a thinly veiled metaphor for locating elements. The two most common ways of describing the direction to elements on the page are called XPath and CSS selector. Let's discuss how absolute and relative paths are used in these two query languages. First we will start with the absolute path.

Using the absolute path

If we write out the absolute path to the **MORE INFO** button we want to click on, we would start from the very top: from the `<html>` tag. Then, we would go into the `<body>` tag, followed by the `<div>` tag, and so on. The fully written out path looks like this in XPath notation:

```
/html/body/div[4]/div[1]/div[4]/div[1]/a[2]
```

> The absolute path for the button written in CSS selector is this (it is just as complicated and ugly as the XPath example):
>
> ```
> html.js body.home.blog.gecko.et_includes_sidebar
> div#main-content-area.container div#special-items.
> clearfix div.special-item div.et-links.clearfix
> a.more-info
> ```

As you can see, when reading from right to left, we are looking for a second link `<a>` that is in the first `<div>` tag of the fourth `<div>` tag and so on, until `<html>` is found. Computers love this type of description, as it is easy to understand: just travel two miles, take the third left, and travel five miles more. But wait a minute, what happens if we add one more new product to the home page? Well, all of the numbers will be off by one and the test will now click on the wrong link. Of course, you did say that you wanted the fourth `<div>` tag and not the fifth after all. Even though using the absolute path is super fast and efficient for the computer, it is rarely used since it is very easy to break. Thus, we use the relative path the majority of the time to find the elements we want.

> Hard coding the position of any element on the page is a poor practice and should be avoided at all costs.

Using the relative path

The best practice to find an element is to use as much contextual information as possible to find the desired element. To accomplish this, we need to start from the closest most unique parent element and drill our way down to the child element that we want. Let's look at a visual step-by-step demonstration:

1. Since the button we are interested in is in the **Special Offers** section, this will become the starting point for the element search.

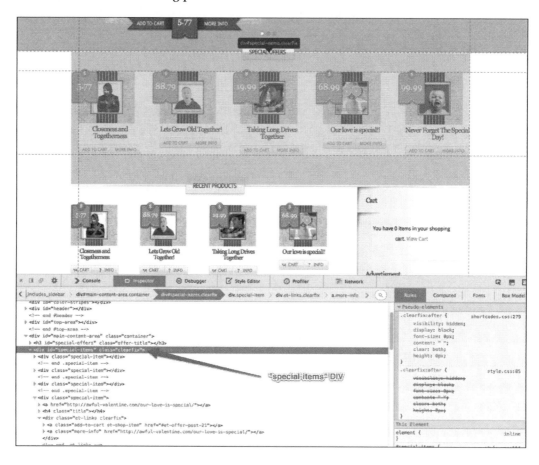

2. Within the `special-items` container, we have four `special-item` products.

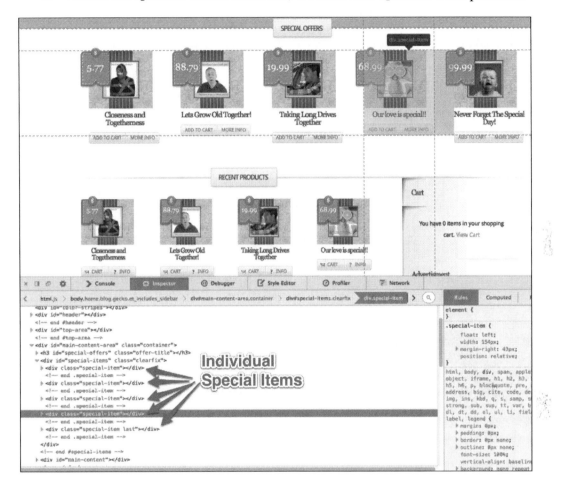

- All of the `special-item` containers have a button with the `more-info` class. Since there are no unique IDs to help us distinguish one product from the other, we look at the target URL for all of the buttons. Once we find the one that should lead us to the correct product, we will click on it.

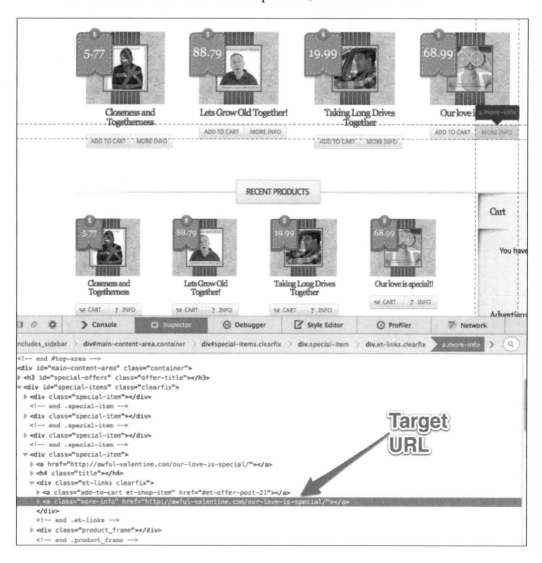

In this example, we started by looking at the grandparent of the desired element and drilling down to the desired child element. XPath and CSS selectors allow reverse traversal from a child element up to the parent element.

Writing locator strategy code

Now that you have a theoretical understanding of the search, let's take a look at a couple of practical examples. We have three ways of implementing the search for the element. When confronted with a similar situation, always choose the approach that is best for the current situation.

 Keep in mind that sometimes one of the approaches will be a lot shorter than the other two. However, the smallest solution that is difficult to understand is always worse than a long solution that is obvious.

Using chained selector strategy methods

Typically, using the `find_element` methods chained in the row is the simplest solution to understand. It is highly verbose, but each individual step is small, concise, and easy to understand compared to a cryptic XPath or CSS selector statement. Let's break down each step of the solution:

```
special_items = selenium.find_elements(:class, "special-item")
```

The first step is to collect all of the `special-item` DIVs, for example:

This will give us an array of possible options. Next, we refine our search by looping through all of the `special-item` DIVs and collecting all the buttons that have the `more-info` class:

```
more_info_buttons = special_items.collect do |special_item|
  special_item.find_element(:class, "more-info")
end
```

The collect method is useful to loop through an existing array and build a new array of selected items.

Finally, we use the find method to loop through the array and pick the button whose href attribute matches the URL of the desired product:

```
button_to_click = more_info_buttons.find do |button|
  button.attribute("href").include?("our-love-is-special")
end
```

Now that we located the **MORE INFO** button, we are ready to click on it!

 The uninterrupted code snipped looks like this:

```
special_items = selenium.find_elements(:class,
"special-item")

more_info_buttons = special_items.collect do
|special_item|
  special_item.find_elements(:class, "more-info")
end

button_to_click = more_info_buttons.find do |button|
  button.attribute("href").include?("our-love-is-
special")
end
```

Using the CSS selector

Looking for the desired element with CSS selector can be accomplished with one line, but it will require basic knowledge of CSS selector syntax:

```
selenium.find_element(:css, '.special-item a[href*="our-love-is-
special"].more-info')
```

In this code snippet, we use the .special-item statement to find all of the special items. We then refine our search to retrieve all of the links with the appropriate href attribute. We finish our search by narrowing down the link list to only the links with the more-info class.

 A very good beginner tutorial for CSS selector is located on the SauceLabs website: https://saucelabs.com/resources/selenium/css-selectors.

Using XPath

In XPath notation, the search query will look like this:

```
selenium.find_element(:xpath, "//div[@class='special-item']//
a[contains(@href, 'our-love-is-special') and @class='more-info']")
```

The `//` symbol in XPath denotes a relative position of elements compared to each other.

>
>
> W3Schools has a detailed XPath tutorial at `http://www.w3schools.com/XPath/`.
>
> When trying to find an element, don't be shy to use any mixture of the mentioned strategies if you need to accomplish the task. Mix and match as much as you need, as long as it is clearly expressed and easy to understand.

Implementing clicks and assertions

Now that we have had a crash course in element locator strategies, we should be able to face any challenge—no matter how difficult it is. Using the CSS selector strategy, we will click on the **MORE INFO** button for our product and check whether we are taken to the correct product page by checking the URL, as shown in the following code:

```
selenium.find_element(:css, '.special-item a[href*="our-love-is-
special"].more-info').click
assert_equal("http://awful-valentine.com/our-love-is-special/",
selenium.current_url)
```

Next, we will use the class locator to get the `category-title` DIV and then check whether the product title matches the expectation:

```
assert_equal("Our love is special!!", selenium.find_element(:class
"category-title").text)
```

Our test file now looks like this:

```
1   require 'rubygems'
2   require 'selenium-webdriver'
3   require 'test/unit'
4
5   class ProductReview < Test::Unit::TestCase
6     def test_add_new_review
7       selenium = Selenium::WebDriver.for(:firefox)
8       selenium.get("http://awful-valentine.com/")
9
10      selenium.find_element(:css, '.special-item a[href*="our-love-is-special"].more-info').click
11      assert_equal("http://awful-valentine.com/our-love-is-special/", selenium.current_url)
12      assert_equal("Our love is special!!", selenium.find_element(:css, ".category-title").text)
13
14      selenium.quit
15    end
16  end
17
18
```

Next, we will add some lines to fill out the product review form and submit the form. We will accomplish this with these seven lines of code:

```
14
15      selenium.find_element(:id, "author").send_keys("Dima")
16      selenium.find_element(:id, "email").send_keys("dima@selenium.com")
17      selenium.find_element(:id, "url").send_keys("http://awful-valentine.com")
18      selenium.find_element(:css, "a[title='5']").click
19      selenium.find_element(:id, "comment").clear
20      selenium.find_element(:id, "comment").send_keys("This is a comment for product #{ENV['USERNAME'] || ENV['USER']}")
21      selenium.find_element(:id, "submit").click
22
```

There are two items of note in preceding code:

- On line **18**, we are using CSS selector strategy to click on the five-star rating for the product.

- On line **20**, we append the computer's username to the comment to make it unique enough to allow the product review to not be rejected by the fraud filter. We will improve this situation in *Chapter 4, Data-driven Testing*.

After the review form is submitted, the product page will refresh and the new review should appear on the page. Time to add some assertions to verify that everything was saved properly.

We could cheat a little and just make an assertion that our semi-unique comment, which we left on the review form, appears somewhere on the page. However, this approach might get us in trouble if an identical comment already exists on the page; our test would not be able to distinguish the existing review from the new one we just created. It is a much better approach to capture the container of the newly created review and check whether each piece of information is correct.

Lucky for us, when a new comment is created, the unique review ID is placed as a hyperlink anchor into the browser's URL. Take a look at this:

Let's use the `selenium.current_url` method to get the URL and parse out the unique review ID:

```
comment_id = selenium.current_url.split("#").last
```

In the preceding code, we are splitting the whole URL string on the hash tag (#) and taking the last item from the resulting array; for me, it was the ninth comment posted to the website so my unique ID is comment-9.

Now that we have a way to pull out just the data we care about, let's store the review container in the review variable so that we can interrogate it later. The code should look like this:

```
22
23        review_id = selenium.current_url.split("#").last
24        review = selenium.find_element(:id, review_id)
25
```

Now let's get the reviewer's name and comment, and then assert the expected value to the actual value:

```
26
27    name = review.find_element(:class, "comment-author-metainfo").find_element(:class, "url").text
28    comment = review.find_element(:class, "comment-content").text
29
30    assert_equal("Dima", name)
31    assert_equal("This is a comment for product #{ENV['USERNAME'] || ENV['USER']}", comment)
32
```

Let's get a little creative; check the date of the newly created comment. We will take a human readable date that looks something like **March 3, 2014 at 3:05 pm** and convert it into a `DateTime` object with the `parse` method. After the parsing is complete, we will use the `Date.today` method call to assert that the timestamp on screen matches today. The code looks like this:

```
31
32    parsed_date = DateTime.parse(review.find_element(:class, "comment-author-metainfo").find_element(:class, "commentmetadata").text)
33    assert_equal(Date.today.year, parsed_date.year)
34    assert_equal(Date.today.month, parsed_date.month)
35    assert_equal(Date.today.day, parsed_date.day)
36
```

Let's take a look at our comment test in its full glory:

```
6 ⊖  def test_add_new_review
7      selenium = Selenium::WebDriver.for(:firefox)
8      selenium.get("http://awful-valentine.com/")
9
10     selenium.find_element(:css, '.special-item a[href*="our-love-is-special"].more-info').click
11     assert_equal("http://awful-valentine.com/our-love-is-special/", selenium.current_url)
12     assert_equal("Our love is special!!", selenium.find_element(:css, ".category-title").text)
13
14
15     selenium.find_element(:id, "author").send_keys("Dima")
16     selenium.find_element(:id, "email").send_keys("dima@selenium.com")
17     selenium.find_element(:id, "url").send_keys("http://awful-valentine.com")
18     selenium.find_element(:css, "a[title='5']").click
19     selenium.find_element(:id, "comment").clear
20     selenium.find_element(:id, "comment").send_keys("This is a comment for product #{ENV['USERNAME'] || ENV['USER']} aa")
21     selenium.find_element(:id, "submit").click
22
23     review_id = selenium.current_url.split("#").last
24     review = selenium.find_element(:id, review_id)
25
26     name = review.find_element(:class, "comment-author-metainfo").find_element(:class, "url").text
27     comment = review.find_element(:class, "comment-content").text
28
29     assert_equal("Dima", name)
30     assert_equal("This is a comment for product #{ENV['USERNAME'] || ENV['USER']} aa", comment)
31
32     parsed_date = DateTime.parse(review.find_element(:class, "comment-author-metainfo").find_element(:class, "commentmetadata").text)
33     assert_equal(Date.today.year, parsed_date.year)
34     assert_equal(Date.today.month, parsed_date.month)
35     assert_equal(Date.today.day, parsed_date.day)
36
37     selenium.quit
38 ⊖ end
```

Duplicating the product review test

Our second test will be a prime example of the Spaghetti pattern. It will completely depend on the first test to set up the test environment and make it ready. The second test is slightly shorter than the first, since it only has one assert at the end. Let's take a look at `test_adding_a_duplicate_review`:

```ruby
def test_adding_a_duplicate_review
  selenium = Selenium::WebDriver.for(:firefox)
  selenium.get("http://awful-valentine.com/")

  selenium.find_element(:css, '.special-item a[href*="our-love-is-special"].more-info').click

  selenium.find_element(:id, "author").send_keys("Dima")
  selenium.find_element(:id, "email").send_keys("dima@selenium.com")
  selenium.find_element(:id, "url").send_keys("http://awful-valentine.com")
  selenium.find_element(:css, "a[title='5']").click
  selenium.find_element(:id, "comment").clear
  selenium.find_element(:id, "comment").send_keys("This is a comment for product #{ENV['USERNAME'] || ENV['USER']} aa")
  selenium.find_element(:id, "submit").click

  error = selenium.find_element(:id, "error-page").text
  assert_equal("Duplicate comment detected; it looks as though you\u2019ve already said that!", error)

  selenium.quit
end
```

Due to the fact that this test relies on unique data, we might need to alter the text that goes into the `comment` text box in order to get the tests to pass during multiple concurrent runs. This is done intentionally to show that data going into the text fields is important and can be extremely difficult to manage.

 We will learn how to properly handle test data in *Chapter 4, Data-driven Testing*.

Reasons for failures

We finished our two tests and we should now examine just how fragile they are. Even though the design of our tests made sense at the time of writing them, they will fail at the slightest provocation. Let's imagine a couple of real-life situations.

The sales team decided that having to change the amount of exclamation marks in the name of the product. These little tweaks happen all the time. We won't change the actual website, but we will change our test to expect a different amount of exclamation marks in the assertion. This will provide a sufficient discrepancy between the test and reality to make the test fail.

 You can download the full test code from `http://awful-valentine.com/code/chapter-2`.

Let's change the assertion in `test_add_new_review` to look like this:

```
assert_equal("Our love is special!!", selenium.find_element(:css, ".category-title").text)

assert_equal("Our love is special!", selenium.find_element(:css, ".category-title").text)
```

Running the tests will now give the following output:

```
Run options:

# Running tests:

FE

Finished tests in 17.082436s, 0.1171 tests/s, 0.1171 assertions/s.

  1) Failure:
test_add_new_review(ProductReview) [test_snippet.rb:14]:
<"Our love is special!"> expected but was
<"Our love is special!!">.

  2) Error:
test_adding_a_duplicate_review(ProductReview):
Selenium::WebDriver::Error::NoSuchElementError: Unable to locate element: {"method":"id","selector":"error-page"}

2 tests, 2 assertions, 1 failures, 1 errors, 0 skips
```

Let's do a postmortem of our tests and list several bad mistakes:

- **Test on test dependence**: This is the most obvious test. If the first test we execute does not complete the review creation process, the environment is not in an ideal state for the second test to run.

- **Hardcoded test data**: Both tests have all of the website implementation details hardcoded. The URL of the product page and the title of the product being tested are written in the test itself. If the any of these details ever change even minutely, we will have to go and update every test that has product data hardcoded. Furthermore, if the product data is different between test environments, these tests cannot be reused. We will discuss test data management in *Chapter 4, Data-driven Testing*.

- **Code duplication**: A lot of actions, such as clicking on links and filling out form data, are duplicated between the tests. We will fix this problem in the next chapter.

All we wanted to do was to test the functionality of the website, and the majority of the choices we made were not obviously bad. However, the end result is a completely unstable test suite. Thus, we inadvertently used an anti-pattern. If uncorrected, our test suite will become so unstable that the whole team will ignore it altogether.

If you are feeling adventurous and want to destabilize our test suite in a couple of other ways, you can experiment with following changes:
1. Delete the first test all together, and only run the second test.
2. Rename the second test to `test_add`.

In both cases, your test suite will fail since the duplication test is not able to recover from its rigid dependencies on the first test.

Before concluding this chapter, let's briefly discuss two other development patterns that are closely related to the Spaghetti pattern. They are not so closely related as to call them siblings, so let's just call them cousins for now. If we wish to make a slight upgrade to our Spaghetti tests, we can convert them to the Chain linked pattern. If we want to downgrade the quality of the test suite, the Big Ball of Mud pattern is a suitable pattern for us.

The Chain Linked pattern

The Chain Linked pattern is an improvement on the Spaghetti pattern. Unlike the bowl of spaghetti, an outstretched length of chain can characterize this pattern. Each link in the chain is an individual test and is an entity on its own. Even though each test is self contained and does not share too much with its neighbors, it still relies on a rigid order of execution. Most tests in this pattern rely on previous tests to set up the environment to be just right. This pattern is a huge improvement on the Spaghetti pattern in its long-term maintainability; however, since the whole test suite needs to be executed every time, it is neither efficient nor easy to use. In conclusion, the Chain Linked pattern might not be the best way to approach writing a test suite. However, it is an overall improvement over the Spaghetti pattern, since it segregates individual tests into more or less self-contained units.

The Big Ball of Mud pattern

Brian Foote and Joseph Yoder first popularized the Big Ball of Mud in their self-titled paper. Unlike the Spaghetti pattern, where the test suite can be separated into individual strands, Big Ball of Mud does not have any formal structures that will allow a distinction between any individual components. Test data and results are promiscuously shared amongst most distant and unrelated components until everything is global and mutable without warning. Unintentional test failures occur when a component is changed for a new test without the realization that hundreds of other tests depend on it. To exacerbate the problem, there is no easy way to find all of the interdependencies since everything is merged together like a piece of wet clay.

Adoption of this pattern is usually unintentional and stems from being developed over long periods of time with different individuals working on different pieces without any overall architectural plan. The initial success of just making it work leads to shortcuts and haphazard patches, which require more and more workarounds just to add one additional feature. In comparison to the Spaghetti pattern, this state of affairs is in much more dire need of repair.

Summary

In this chapter, we added two new tests to our test suite. In order to do that, we had to first learn some advanced techniques of locating elements on the page; no matter how complicated the website might be, we can now test it! By the end of the chapter, we had two tests that heavily depended on each other; we watched them crash and burn at the slightest problem. We then analyzed the shortcomings of the Spaghetti pattern and briefly talked about the two related anti-patterns: the Chain Linked pattern and the Big Ball of Mud.

In the next chapter, we will refactor our test suite to dry out our code. We will make our tests more independent and stable by decoupling them from the implementation details and each other.

3
Refactoring Tests

"A bear, however hard he tries,
Grows tubby without exercise...."

- A. A. Milne, "Teddy Bear" from The Complete Poems of Winnie-the-Pooh

Exercise is an important part of keeping your body fit; however, it can be easily despised. Exercising takes a lot of work, causes a lot of physical pain, and gives very few instant results to keep you motivated. Our test suite needs some upkeep and refactoring to remain in pristine condition.

In the previous chapter, we wrote two tests but we did it in a quick and sloppy manner. A lot of code was duplicated, and simply copied and pasted. If we keep growing our suite in a similar manner, it will become unmanageable in no time! In this chapter, we will put our test suite on a treadmill to get it into a better overall shape. We will cover the following topics:

- Refactoring tests
- The DRY principle
- The DRY testing pattern
- Setup and teardown methods
- The Hermetic test pattern
- Test independence
- Using timestamps to create unique test data
- Sharing common functionalities between tests
- Random run order practice

Refactoring tests

Since this chapter will be focused on refactoring tests, let's first define this term. Refactoring is the act of restructuring your code to improve the internal efficiency, stability, and long-term maintainability without adding or modifying any of the underlying functionalities. At the end of the refactoring session, we should not have any new tests; the only goal is to improve the existing tests.

Since there are no obvious instant results such as having 10 more new tests, refactoring may seem like a waste of time. However, having two tests that do not randomly fail is a lot more productive in the long run than having 12 tests that cannot be relied on. Refactoring your tests is similar to calisthenics; if you don't exercise, you will probably die of a heart attack 20 years before your time. That being said, we will not add any new tests in this chapter. Instead, we will improve the product review tests in *Chapter 2*, *The Spaghetti Pattern*.

The DRY testing pattern

Treating automated tests with the same care and respect as the application that we are trying to test is the key to long-term success. Adopting common software development principles and design patterns will prevent some costly maintenance in the future. One of these principles is the **Don't Repeat Yourself (DRY)** principle; the most basic idea behind the DRY principle is to reduce long-term maintenance costs by removing all unnecessary duplication.

> There are a few times when it is okay to have a duplicate code, at least temporarily. As Donald Knuth so eloquently stated, "Premature optimization is the root of all evil (or at least most of it) in programming."

The DRY testing pattern embraces the DRY principle and expands on it. Not only do we remove the duplicate code and duplicate test implementations, but we also remove duplicate test goals.

> A test goal or test target is the main idea behind any given test. The rule of thumb is if you cannot describe what the test is supposed to accomplish in a sentence or two, then the test is too complicated or it does not understand what it is testing. A good example of a test goal would be "an anonymous user should be able to purchase product X on the website."

We are trying to avoid accidentally testing any functionality not related to the current test. For example, if the target of the current test is the registration flow, this test should not fail if a social media icon fails to load. Social media icons should have a test of their own that is not related to registration tests.

 David Thomas and Andrew Hunt formulated the DRY principle in their book, *The Pragmatic Programmer*, by Andrew Hunt and David Thomas, published by *Addison-Wesley Professional*. The DRY principle is sometimes referred to as **Single Source Of Truth (SSOT)** or **Single Point Of Truth (SPOT)** because it attempts to store every single piece of unique information in one place only.

Advantages of the DRY testing pattern

Writing tests using the DRY testing pattern has many advantages. Here are four advantages:

- **Modular tests**: Tests and test implementations are self-sufficient. Any test can run in any order. Also, test actions such as clicking or registering a new user are shared during the tests.

- **Reduced duplication**: All actions such as filling out a form are neatly kept in a single place instead of having multiple copies peppered all over the suite.

- **Fast updates**: Having unique actions in a single place makes it easy to update the tests to mimic new growth of the application.

- **No junk code**: Constant upkeep of the test suite, with deletion of duplicates, prevents the test suite from having code that is no longer used.

Disadvantages of the DRY testing pattern

There are some disadvantages of setting your tests according to the DRY testing pattern; it is a lot of work and requires a lot of buy in from the whole team. Here are some of the most common issues:

- **Complicated project structure**: Some test actions will be logically grouped with other similar actions. Filling out a login form and clicking the login button will probably happen in the same implementation file. However, some actions will inevitably end up in a different file, making it hard to find them.

- **Lack of a good IDE**: There aren't many good IDEs that will notify the test developer if a test action has already been implemented. Most test developers will reimplement the action they need instead of looking for it.

 The best way around this problem is to have a lot of in-team communication. Asking whether anyone has already implemented an action in code will save you time and prevent duplication.

- **Constant upkeep**: Keeping the test suite clean and applying the DRY test pattern will need dedication from the team. Duplicate code needs to be pruned and deleted instead of being ignored.

 In statically typed languages such as Java, we can use static analysis tools that can be used to monitor code duplication.

- **Programming skills**: This needs to be improved by the whole team. One test developer who keeps duplicating logic and cargo-culting can spoil the elegant test suite in a matter of weeks.

 Cargo cult is a phrase commonly used to describe a programming style where a programmer uses a piece of code without understanding what the original intention of that code was. It can be described as "we do this because we always did this; I don't know why."

Let's start DRY-ing out our tests. The first and obvious choice is the setup and teardown methods.

Moving code into a setup and teardown

Most modern testing frameworks include the concept of a setup and teardown. Each framework can call them by a different name. For example, in Cucumber, the setup is called `Background`, while in Rspec, it is called `Before`. No matter what name the framework chooses, the idea behind these two methods remains the same. This setup is run before tests and is used to get the environment in a test-ready state. The teardown is used to clean up after the tests to put the environment back into a pristine state. Some frameworks allow the setup and teardown to be run before and after each individual test, while others only allow them to be executed before and after a group of tests; some even allow both.

Let's start cleaning up `product_review_test.rb` from *Chapter 2, The Spaghetti Pattern,* by adding the `setup` and `teardown` methods:

 You can find the complete `product_review_test.rb` file at `http://awful-valentine.com/code/chapter-2/`.

1. The first thing we will do is add the `setup` and `teardown` methods at the top of our test; our code will look like this:

```
1    require 'rubygems'
2    require 'selenium-webdriver'
3    require 'test/unit'
4
5    class ProductReview < Test::Unit::TestCase
6
7        def setup
8
9        end
10
11       def teardown
12
13       end
14
```

2. Let's move the creation of the Firefox instance into `setup` and the quitting of the Firefox instance into `teardown`, as seen in the following screenshot:

```
1    require 'rubygems'
2    require '@selenium-webdriver'
3    require 'test/unit'
4
5    class ProductReview < Test::Unit::TestCase
6
7        def setup
8            @selenium = @selenium::WebDriver.for(:firefox)    ⬅
9        end
10
11       def teardown
12           @selenium.quit   ⬅
13       end
14
15       def test_add_new_review
16           @selenium.get("http://awful-valentine.com/")
17
18           @selenium.find_element(:css, '.special-item a[href*="our-love-is-special"].more-info').click
19           assert_equal("http://awful-valentine.com/our-love-is-special/", @selenium.current_url)
20           # assert_equal("Our love is special!!", @selenium.find_element(:css, ".category-title").text)
```

We changed all instances of the selenium variable to `@selenium`; this makes our variable an instance variable for the current test class. Individual tests are now able to reference the `@selenium` variable instead of having to create their own.

Our tests are starting to look better right away; the setup method is helping us to create a new instance of Firefox before each test is started. The biggest advantage is that the `teardown` method will execute every single time the test finishes. This means that Firefox will be closed every time, even if the test fails before completion.

Removing duplication with methods

Let's keep refactoring our test's logic; the next item to refactor is the click on the home page for the product we desire to comment on. Let's create a new method called `select_desired_product_on_homepage`, and move the `click` code inside it, as seen here:

```
11  def teardown
12    @selenium.quit
13  end
14
15  def select_desired_product_on_homepage
16    @selenium.find_element(:css, '.special-item a[href*="our-love-is-special"].more-info').click
17  end
18
```

After we move the `click` action to the new method, we need to invoke this method from our test, like this:

```
15  def select_desired_product_on_homepage
16    @selenium.find_element(:css, '.special-item a[href*="our-love-is-special"].more-info').click
17  end
18
19  def test_add_new_review
20    @selenium.get("http://awful-valentine.com/")
21
22    select_desired_product_on_homepage
23    assert_equal("http://awful-valentine.com/our-love-is-special/", @selenium.current_url)
24    assert_equal("Our love is special!!", @selenium.find_element(:css, ".category-title").text)
25
```

We need to perform the same refactoring in the `test_adding_a_duplicate_review` test. This way, both tests use the same method call to select a product on the home page.

Removing external test goals

In the previous chapter, we added two assertions; they were there to verify that clicking on the **MORE INFO** link on the home page takes us to the correct product. The assertions are shown here:

```
19  def test_add_new_review
20      @selenium.get("http://awful-valentine.com/")
21
22      select_desired_product_on_homepage
23   ➤  assert_equal("http://awful-valentine.com/our-love-is-special/", @selenium.current_url)
24   ➤  assert_equal("Our love is special!!", @selenium.find_element(:css, ".category-title").text)
25
```

These do not adhere to the DRY testing pattern, because the tests are no longer testing the product review functionalities; now they also test the product retrieval and display functionalities.

Besides performing duplicate assertions, they make the test suite unstable. Test that check product review functionality broke because of a minor editorial change to the page content. The most logical thing to do is delete this instability causing code and write a set of tests specifically to test product descriptions. We will delete the assertions now and add the new tests in *Chapter 4, Data-driven Testing*.

Let's take a look at the test after we delete the unnecessary assertions:

```
19  def test_add_new_review
20      @selenium.get("http://awful-valentine.com/")
21                                                      Assertions used to be here
22      select_desired_product_on_homepage    ⬅
23
24      @selenium.find_element(:id, "author").send_keys("Dima")
25      @selenium.find_element(:id, "email").send_keys("dima@selenium.com")
26      @selenium.find_element(:id, "url").send_keys("http://awful-valentine.com")
27      @selenium.find_element(:css, "a[title='5']").click
28      @selenium.find_element(:id, "comment").clear
```

Using a method to fill out the review form

Finally, the biggest chunk of duplication comes from filling out the review form. Since the values that we insert in the form fields are identical between the two tests, we should be able to easily pull out this duplication to `fill_out_comment_form`. Our new method will look like this:

```
def fill_out_comment_form
  @selenium.find_element(:id, "author").send_keys("Dima")
  @selenium.find_element(:id, "email").send_keys("dima@@selenium.com")
  @selenium.find_element(:id, "url").send_keys("http://awful-valentine.com")
  @selenium.find_element(:css, "a[title='5']").click
  @selenium.find_element(:id, "comment").clear
  @selenium.find_element(:id, "comment").send_keys("This is a comment for product #{ENV['USERNAME'] || ENV['USER']} aa")
  @selenium.find_element(:id, "submit").click
end
```

Reviewing the refactored code

Our tests are starting to look completely different from when we first began refactoring. In the book *Refactoring to Patterns*, the author *Joshua Kerievsky*, shows readers how to refactor code into a series of small, easy-to-understand actions. The idea is to avoid refactoring the whole class or file in one go. We might have an idea of how the code is supposed to look when we are finished with it, but rewriting everything into its final form right away tends to prove difficult. So, it is better to take many tiny steps than one giant step that will often leave us confused and frustrated.

 Refactoring to Patterns by *Joshua Kerievsky*, published by *Addison-Wesley Professional*.

Staying with the principle of small, easy-to-understand changes, let's review our test code so far before we make any more modifications to it. First, let's take a look at the four new methods we added.

```
1   require 'rubygems'
2   require '@selenium-webdriver'
3   require 'test/unit'
4
5   class ProductReview < Test::Unit::TestCase
6
7       def setup
8         @selenium = @selenium::WebDriver.for(:firefox)
9       end
10
11      def teardown
12        @selenium.quit
13      end
14
15      def select_desired_product_on_homepage
16        @selenium.find_element(:css, '.special-item a[href*="our-love-is-special"].more-info').click
17      end
18
19      def fill_out_comment_form
20        @selenium.find_element(:id, "author").send_keys("Dima")
21        @selenium.find_element(:id, "email").send_keys("dima@@selenium.com")
22        @selenium.find_element(:id, "url").send_keys("http://awful-valentine.com")
23        @selenium.find_element(:css, "a[title='5']").click
24        @selenium.find_element(:id, "comment").clear
25        @selenium.find_element(:id, "comment").send_keys("This is a comment for product #{ENV['USERNAME'] || ENV['USER']} aa")
26        @selenium.find_element(:id, "submit").click
27      end
28
```

Everything should look familiar so far. The `setup` and `teardown` methods run before
and after each test and manage the instances of Selenium WebDriver and Firefox.
The `select_desired_product_on_homepage` method can be invoked on the home
page to click on the **MORE INFO** button for the product we want to review. Finally,
the `fill_out_comment_form` method fills out the review form for the product
we've selected.

Next, let's take a look at `test_add_new_review`, shown here:

```
49
50      def test_adding_a_duplicate_review
51        @selenium.get("http://awful-valentine.com/")
52
53        select_desired_product_on_homepage
54        fill_out_comment_form
55
56        error = @selenium.find_element(:id, "error-page").text
57        assert_equal("Duplicate comment detected; it looks as though you\u2019ve already said that!", error)
58      end
59   end
60
```

So far, we have dramatically improved the code quality of our tests. By moving out some of the duplication into individual methods, we made our test suite a lot easier to maintain in the long run. The `select_desired_product_on_homepage` and `fill_out_comment_form` methods can now be reused by any test in our test class. This means that if we ever need to update our test to adhere to the new functionalities, we only need to do it once in the appropriate method; all of the tests will automatically work.

Since we are extremely dedicated to having a good test suite, we will not stop refactoring just yet. Our next goal is to fix test instability caused by the Spaghetti pattern; we will break the test-on-test dependency in the next section.

Make sure you fully understand all of the actions performed so far before moving on to the next section.

The Hermetic test pattern

The Hermetic test pattern is the polar opposite of the Spaghetti pattern; it states that each test should be completely independent and self-sufficient. Any dependency on other tests or third-party services that cannot be controlled should be avoided at all costs. It is impossible to get a perfectly hermetically sealed test; however, anytime a dependency on anything outside the test is detected, it should be removed as soon as possible.

The Hermetic test pattern can also be referred to as **Test is an Island Pattern**, which is a play on the word from an old saying *no man is an island*.

Advantages of the Hermetic test pattern

The Hermetic pattern is especially appealing when trying to flush out test instability. Here are some advantages to hermetically seal your tests:

- **Clean start**: Each test has a cleaned up environment to work in. This prevents accidental test pollution from previous tests, such as a created user that should not be present.

- **Resilience**: Each test is responsible for its own environment, so it has no need for everything to go perfectly right somewhere else in the suite.

We will talk about data management for individual tests in *Chapter 4, Data-driven Testing*.

- **Modular**: Each test is standalone and can be rearranged into smaller test suites such as a smoke suite, or can run as a standalone test.

 Smoke suite refers to a set of smoke tests, which is run on any environment, usually immediately post deploy of a new version. The idea is to quickly smoke out any issues in the new build. Other types of test suites are discussed in *Chapter 8, Growing the Test Suite*.

- **Random run order practice**: Since tests do not depend on successful completion of any other test in the suite, they can be executed in any order. We'll cover more on random run order practice later in this chapter.

- **Parallel testing**: If our test suite can run in any random execution order, it can also be executed in parallel. Executing multiple tests simultaneously can significantly reduce the runtime of the test suite.

Disadvantages of the Hermetic test pattern

Hermetically sealing each test comes with an increase in individual test stability but it does have some disadvantages:

- **Upfront design**: Each test needs to be designed to be self-sufficient. Each test can reuse methods used by other tests, but cannot reuse data and test results generated by other tests.

- **Runtime increase**: Since each test has to set up the environment before it starts, the runtime of each individual test is increased.

 This effect is easily negated when the test suite is executed in parallel.

- **Resource usage increase**: Increased runtime of individual tests means that the test suite will need more resources, such as RAM, to run tests in parallel.

Removing test-on-test dependence

In the previous chapter, we created two tests; one of which depended on the success of the first test for the environment to be in a testable state. So far, we removed some of the duplication from our tests but we did not solve the data interdependency. You may have probably noticed that running our tests multiple times in a row will fail tests in unpredictable ways unless you constantly update the test data manually in between the test runs. In this section, we will make our tests independent of hardcoded test data and each other.

Our website only checks that the content of the comment is unique; it does not check whether any of the other fields such as name are duplicates. So, we can modify our test to provide a new comment every time the `fill_out_comment_form` method is called by passing in the comment we want to add:

```
18
19   def fill_out_comment_form(comment)
20       @selenium.find_element(:id, "author").send_keys("Dima")
21       @selenium.find_element(:id, "email").send_keys("dima@@selenium.com")
22       @selenium.find_element(:id, "url").send_keys("http://awful-valentine.com")
23       @selenium.find_element(:css, "a[title='5']").click
24       @selenium.find_element(:id, "comment").clear
25       @selenium.find_element(:id, "comment").send_keys(comment)
26       @selenium.find_element(:id, "submit").click
27   end
28
```

Our `fill_out_comment_form` method now accepts comment text from the test, so we can make our test generate a unique comment and pass it to the `fill_out_comment_form` method.

Using timestamps as test data

Using timestamps to guarantee unique data is a great shortcut when writing tests, since it is very unlikely that two tests will be executed at the exact same time. Let's create a method that will generate a unique comment by adding a timestamp to it, as follows:

```
28
29   def generate_unique_comment
30       "This is a comment for product and is for #{Time.now.to_i}"
31   end
32
```

> In Ruby, the last statement in a method is automatically returned; so, having `return` is redundant in this case.

What makes our `generate_unique_comment` method work is the `Time.now.to_i` call, which returns a timestamp in seconds since the epoch.

> Epoch is a UNIX timestamp of seconds elapsed since January 1, 1970.

If we were to print out our unique comment with the timestamp, it would look something like this:

Let's add a new variable to our test, which will generate and store the unique comments, so that we can use it later in the test when we perform an assertion. Our code will look like this with the new variable pointed out with arrows:

```ruby
def test_add_new_review
    @selenium.get("http://awful-valentine.com/")

    select_desired_product_on_homepage
    unique_comment = generate_unique_comment
    fill_out_comment_form(unique_comment)

    review_id = @selenium.current_url.split("#").last
    review = @selenium.find_element(:id, review_id)

    name = review.find_element(:class, "comment-author-metainfo").find_element(:class, "url").text
    comment = review.find_element(:class, "comment-content").text

    assert_equal("Dima", name)
    assert_equal(unique_comment, comment)

    parsed_date = DateTime.parse(review.find_element(:class, "comment-author-metainfo").find_element(:class, "commentmetadata").text)
    assert_equal(Date.today.year, parsed_date.year)
    assert_equal(Date.today.month, parsed_date.month)
    assert_equal(Date.today.day, parsed_date.day)
end
```

Extracting the remaining common actions to methods

Now that we got the pesky data uniqueness out of the way, we can refactor our tests even further! Currently, our `test_add_new_review` test fills out a product review every single time it runs. At the same time, our `test_adding_a_duplicate_review` test relies on that review to exist before the actual assertion can take place. Since both tests are using the same functionalities to create a product review, we can extract and reuse duplicate code between the tests by extracting it to a method and having both tests call the said method.

Creating a new review with a single method call

Here are the four actions that both of our tests share:

- **Navigating to the home page**: The starting point of both of the tests is to get to the home page. The rest of the execution starts from this point.

- **Select product**: A given product needs to be selected and the **MORE INFO** button needs to be clicked, so that we can review the product.

- **New review form completion**: Both tests fill out the product review form with identical data.

- **Retrieve new review ID**: After the review is created, the review ID is retrieved for double assertion.

 This step is optional for the duplicate review test, since it does not actually do anything with the review ID.

We need to create a new method that can easily be called by both the tests. To make the `generate_new_product_review` method portable and reusable, we will not implement the previously described tests in it. Instead, we will create several helper methods that the `generate_new_product_review` method will call. First, let's create a method to navigate to the home page, as shown here:

```
def navigate_to_homepage
  @selenium.get("http://awful-valentine.com/")
end
```

We already have the methods to select a product on the home page and fill out the review form; so we will skip those. Let's make a method to retrieve the newly generated review ID now; get_newly_created_review_id is shown as follows:

```
def get_newly_created_review_id
  @selenium.current_url.split("#").last
end
```

Let's pull together all of these methods into generate_new_product_review like this:

```
def generate_new_product_review(review)
  navigate_to_homepage
  select_desired_product_on_homepage
  fill_out_comment_form(review)
  get_newly_created_review_id
end
```

As mentioned earlier, Ruby implicitly adds the return statement to the very last action in any method. This means that the generate_new_product_review method will automatically give the returned value of the get_newly_created_review_id method, which happens to be the new review comment.

Let's take a look at `test_add_new_review` after we finish this round of refactoring. It will look like this:

```
def test_add_new_review
  unique_comment = generate_unique_comment
  review_id = generate_new_product_review(unique_comment)

  review = @selenium.find_element(:id, review_id)

  name = review.find_element(:class, "comment-author-metainfo").find_element(:class, "url").text
  comment = review.find_element(:class, "comment-content").text

  assert_equal("Dima", name)
  assert_equal(unique_comment, comment)

  parsed_date = DateTime.parse(review.find_element(:class, "comment-author-metainfo").find_element(:class, "commentmetadata").text)
  assert_equal(Date.today.year, parsed_date.year)
  assert_equal(Date.today.month, parsed_date.month)
  assert_equal(Date.today.day, parsed_date.day)
end
```

Our test now generates a unique comment, passes that comment to review a generation method, and uses the returned `review_id` to collect the needed information for assertions. Let's take a look at `test_adding_a_duplicate_review` now:

```
def test_adding_a_duplicate_review
  unique_comment = generate_unique_comment
  generate_new_product_review(unique_comment)
  sleep 10
  generate_new_product_review(unique_comment)

  error = @selenium.find_element(:id, "error-page").text
  assert_equal("Duplicate comment detected; it looks as though you\u2019ve already said that!", error)
end
```

The duplicate review test benefits the most from this refactoring. At this point, it has to call the `generate_new_product_review` method two times in a row to be ready for assertions. This test is now completely independent. Even if `test_add_new_review` never runs, it will still be able to test duplicate review functionalities.

 Note that we added `sleep 10` (denoted with an arrow) in our duplicate review test. The product review form has another fraud detection mechanism, which prevents users from posting product reviews too rapidly. The `sleep 10` call will allow 10 seconds to elapse between review creations to work around this limitation.

Reviewing the test-on-test dependency refactoring

As we did before, let's review our refactoring session progress. The `setup` and `teardown` methods have not changed at all.

```
1   require 'rubygems'
2   require '@selenium-webdriver'
3   require 'test/unit'
4
5   class ProductReview < Test::Unit::TestCase
6
7     def setup
8       @selenium = @selenium::WebDriver.for(:firefox)
9     end
10
11    def teardown
12      @selenium.quit
13    end
14
```

 The order of method declarations has changed to make the test class more aesthetically pleasing to read.

The two tests for the product review functionalities look like this:

```
14
15  def test_add_new_review
16    unique_comment = generate_unique_comment
17    review_id = generate_new_product_review(unique_comment)
18
19    review = @selenium.find_element(:id, review_id)
20
21    name = review.find_element(:class, "comment-author-metainfo").find_element(:class, "url").text
22    comment = review.find_element(:class, "comment-content").text
23
24    assert_equal("Dima", name)
25    assert_equal(unique_comment, comment)
26
27    parsed_date = DateTime.parse(review.find_element(:class, "comment-author-metainfo").find_element(:class, "commentmetadata").text)
28    assert_equal(Date.today.year, parsed_date.year)
29    assert_equal(Date.today.month, parsed_date.month)
30    assert_equal(Date.today.day, parsed_date.day)
31  end
32
33  def test_adding_a_duplicate_review
34    unique_comment = generate_unique_comment
35    generate_new_product_review(unique_comment)
36    sleep 10
37    generate_new_product_review(unique_comment)
38
39    error = @selenium.find_element(:id, "error-page").text
40    assert_equal("Duplicate comment detected; it looks as though you\u2019ve already said that!", error)
41  end
42
```

Finally, all of the refactored out helper methods are moved into the private section of the test class, as follows:

```ruby
42
43      private
44
45      def select_desired_product_on_homepage
46        @selenium.find_element(:css, '.special-item a[href*="our-love-is-special"].more-info').click
47      end
48
49      def generate_new_product_review(review)
50        navigate_to_homepage
51        select_desired_product_on_homepage
52        fill_out_comment_form(review)
53        get_newly_created_review_id
54      end
55
56      def fill_out_comment_form(comment)
57        @selenium.find_element(:id, "author").send_keys("Dima")
58        @selenium.find_element(:id, "email").send_keys("dima@@selenium.com")
59        @selenium.find_element(:id, "url").send_keys("http://awful-valentine.com")
60        @selenium.find_element(:css, "a[title='5']").click
61        @selenium.find_element(:id, "comment").clear
62        @selenium.find_element(:id, "comment").send_keys(comment)
63        @selenium.find_element(:id, "submit").click
64      end
65
66      def navigate_to_homepage
67        @selenium.get("http://awful-valentine.com/")
68      end
69
70      def generate_unique_comment
71        "This is a comment for product and is for #{Time.now.to_i}"
72      end
73
74      def get_newly_created_review_id
75        @selenium.current_url.split("#").last
76      end
```

Creating generic DRY methods

At this point, our test is no longer recognizable compared to what it was at the beginning of the chapter. Before we wrap it up, let's talk about the generic action used all through our tests. Throughout the test code, we use some common methods to perform actions such as clicking or typing text into a text field. These chained methods look something like this:

```ruby
@selenium.find_element(:id, "url").send_keys("http://awful-valentine.com")
```

What if we refactor these methods a little further and create some generic private methods that can be used in a much simpler way? Let's start with the most common method used, `@selenium.find_element`, and create a generic `find_element` method:

```
def find_element(element, strategy=:css)
  @selenium.find_element(strategy, element)
end
```

Our `find_element` method now accepts an `element` identifier and an optional `strategy` parameter. If the strategy is not specified, it will default to the CSS selector.

 More information about element locator strategies can be found in *Chapter 2, The Spaghetti Pattern.*

Now let's add two new methods that use our local `find_element` method to click and type text into text fields. These methods look like this.

```
def type_text(text, element, strategy=:css)
  find_element(element, strategy).send_keys(text)
end

def click(element, strategy=:css)
  find_element(element, strategy).click
end
```

Refactoring with generic methods

Now that we have three very generic methods that allow tests to interact with the web page, you have a small homework assignment. Finish refactoring the rest of the test, and see how many more generic methods you can create. I'll give you a hint; the `fill_out_comment_form` method from earlier now looks something like this:

```
def fill_out_comment_form(comment)
  type_text("Dima", "author", :id)
  type_text("dima@@selenium.com", "email", :id)
  type_text("http://awful-valentine.com", "url", :id)
  click("a[title='5']")
  find_element("comment", :id).clear
  type_text(comment, "comment", :id)
  click("submit", :id)
end
```

We will take greater advantage of generic action methods when we get to the *The Action Wrapper pattern* section in *Chapter 5, Stabilizing the Tests*.

Before we finish this chapter, let's take a look at the random run order principle, which takes advantage of the refactoring we just completed. Without all of this work, we would never be able to put this principle into practice.

The random run order principle

Random run order is more of a principle than a pattern. It applies to the test execution. This execution is usually performed on a **Continuous Integration** (**CI**) environment. The random run order principle states that the order of the test suite execution should be randomized every time the suite is executed. The idea is to flush out instabilities in the test suite by introducing an element of chaos. Any test that has a hidden dependency on another test will eventually fail when the test run order is random.

CI tools are simple applications that execute a given build when certain conditions such as code change are met. There are several commercial tools available, such as **TeamCity**, **Bamboo**, and **Travis-CI**. One of the most popular and free open source CI tools is **Jenkins**, which can be found at `http://jenkins-ci.org/`.

Advantages of the random run order principle

Let's talk about the advantages of running our tests in a random order:

- **Prevents test interdependence**: Any test that depends on another test to set up the environment will be exposed rather quickly. This forces us to maintain good Hermetic integrity within each test.

The type of test-on-test dependency described here is the Chain Linked pattern, discussed in *Chapter 2, The Spaghetti Pattern*.

- **Flushes out data pollution**: Sometimes test flakiness does not come from the setup stage of the test. Often we will find a test that intentionally puts the test environment into a bad state on purpose, to test the application resilience. If the said test leaves the environment in a bad state after completion, it can break the test that follows.

 Ideally, each test will set up the test environment in the setup stage of the execution, and return the environment to the original state every single time in the teardown stage.

- **Built in**: Some test frameworks not only support test randomization out of the box, but also have the random run order as a default setting.

Disadvantages of the random run order principle

As always, there are some negatives when making your test suite compatible with the random run order; here is a short list:

- **A lot of refactoring**: If we have a large and mature test suite with copious usage of the Spaghetti pattern and the Big Ball of Mud pattern, making tests compatible with a random run order is tremendous amount of work.

- **Random run audits**: If the test run is completely random for every single build, it can be difficult to know the sequence of tests that causes the instability. One way to solve this difficulty is to have an audit trail for each build that will allow us to know the exact sequence of tests that led us to failure.

- **Team frustration**: Running tests in a random order can create a lot of frustration and resentment for the whole team. When working on a deadline, having your build fail due to unrelated data pollution is annoying.

 Remember that to go fast, one needs to start slow. Issues like these will always slow down the whole process initially. Once they are exposed and fixed, the overall velocity of the test development actually goes up.

- **No built-in support**: A lot of test frameworks do not support test randomization. Implementing this functionality might be very difficult.

Summary

In this chapter, we discussed the harmful effects of code duplication on the test suite. As the application keeps evolving, the time required to keep the tests up to date grows exponentially. The solution for this is to avoid code and test duplication by using the DRY testing pattern. We applied the DRY principle by refactoring duplicate code into the `setup` and `teardown` methods and other methods that our tests can share.

We also removed the interdependency between our two tests by using the Hermetic test pattern. Removing the Spaghetti pattern from our suite has dramatically increased the test stability. Random order ability was achieved by hermetically sealing our tests and having them use unique data.

In the next chapter, we will be concentrating on test data and how to manage it in different environments.

4
Data-driven Testing

"Errors using inadequate data are much less than those using no data at all."

-Charles Babbage

Test data is a crucial part of automated tests; the old truism *garbage in, garbage out* applies especially well in this case. Tests will feed some data into our Turing machine and compare the output with the expectations. In a manner of speaking, a perfect test is a little insane; it will keep doing the same things over and over while expecting a different result.

As automated test developers, our goal is to make the tests fulfill their destiny of endlessly repeating identical steps, forever. The only way to accomplish this goal is to have as much control as possible over every single piece of data our application consumes. Test data is not just the text our test will type into the purchase form; test data is the complete state of the whole environment we are testing. In this chapter, we will take control of the environment we are testing by using these concepts:

- Fixtures
- Stubs
- YAML
- JSON
- Using API endpoints
- Generating test cases with a loop
- The default values pattern
- The faker library

Data relevance versus data accessibility

Controlling the test data, or the state of our environment, is a continuous battle of how relevant our data is versus how easily accessible it is. Relevance is a scale of how closely our environment mimics our production environment. Accessibility is a scale of how easy it is to control the data in a given environment. Each of the environments we will test will fall somewhere in between these two scales. The following graph is a rough representation of this idea:

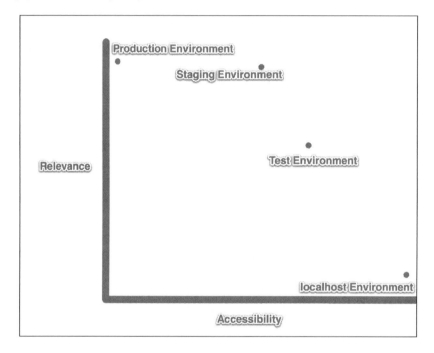

In this graph, points higher up on the y axis mimic production data the closest. Conversely, the lower points do not resemble production at all. The x axis represents the ability to have control on our data and environment, with the rightmost point having full control and leftmost point having close to zero control.

Testing our application on a localhost will yield some of the most consistent results, as we have full and total control over every variable. But this comes at a cost; our tests may be missing bugs since we might not be able to use real production data, or simulate production like load on the website. Running tests against the production environment is generally frowned upon, since our tests will fill up the database with fake usernames. Worse still, they might be making test purchases in your store!

Never write a Selenium test to make real currency purchases on your production website; if you choose to disobey this rule, at least make sure not to leave your personal credit card information in the test for all to see! We will now try to resolve this delicate balance of data we can and cannot control between the different environments. A very good starting point is to extract as much of the test data out of the test implementation as possible.

Hardcoding input data

Hardcoding test data is just like hardcoding anything in a software; a quick and dirty fix that will forever haunt your nightmares. In *Chapter 3*, *Refactoring Tests*, we refactored out some bad practices from our tests. We, however, left test data still hardcoded in the tests. Let's take a look at how each piece of the test data can make our life difficult:

- **URL of the website**: Like most web projects, we have several testing environments: staging, localhost, development, and so on. Our tests have the URL of the application hardcoded; thus, without changing the test code, we cannot have the tests execute on both the staging and production environments.

- **Hardcoded product**: Typically, different test environments do not share the same identical data such as products. Furthermore, most environments will only have a subset of the products available in production. Test environments in particular will have products that never did and never will exist in production.

- **Private user data**: Due to legal reasons, our test environment should never contain user data from the production environment. This is doubly true for sensitive user information, such as credit card numbers and e-mails.

Our test should be able to, within reason, run on any environment we have. But this is not possible if every single piece of data we use is hardcoded for a test environment.

Hiding test data from tests

The act of hiding data from tests sounds counterintuitive at first; the tests need to do things with the data after all. To make our tests flexible enough to work on any test environment we want, we will need to provide them with data applicable to the said environment. However, the test itself does not need to know what data we are using. When the data is properly hidden, the test does not care what username and password is used; the information fed into the test from the outside is stored as a variable.

To start hiding our data, we will need a single place that stores data and provides it to the test on request. For this, we will create a new class called `TestData` in the `test_data.rb` file. Let's create this file and add an empty class inside it:

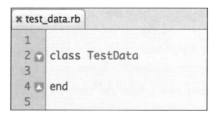

The first variable we want to move into the `TestData` class is the URL of the website we are testing. It is the simplest and fastest way to start adding this functionality. Let's take a look at the `get_base_url` method we created:

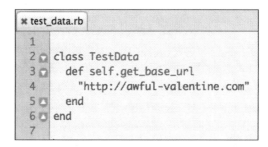

Now that we have a simple way to get the URL of our test environment, all we have to do is call `TestData.get_base_url` from anywhere in the test. We are ready to hide the test environment URL from the tests.

 The naming convention of the `get_base_url` method is slightly different from before; it now begins with a keyword, `self`. By adding `self` in front of a method name, we turn it into a class method (static method), which will allow us to call it directly without first creating a new instance of the `TestData` object.

Let's modify the `product_review_test.rb` file; we will need to tell our test to include the code from `test_data.rb`, making the `TestData` class accessible.

 The `File.dirname(__FILE__)` call is used to locate the current relative directory of our test file, and `File.join` is used to join the relative path with a file called `test_data`.

The code in the following screenshot shows how to require another Ruby file such as `test_data.rb`:

```
✖ product_review_test.rb
1   require 'rubygems'
2   require 'selenium-webdriver'
3   require 'test/unit'
4   require File.join(File.dirname(__FILE__), 'test_data')
5
```

Part of the refactoring effort in *Chapter 3, Refactoring Tests*, was to create the `navigate_to_homepage` method. Both of the tests in `product_review_test.rb` use this method, so we only need to modify our code in one place to start using the `TestData` class. Without the DRY principle, we would have to locate every test that navigated to the home page and modify the URL. Instead, our modification simply looks like this:

```
def navigate_to_homepage
  @selenium.get(TestData.get_base_url)
end
```

We have successfully obfuscated the URL of the environment from the test. As always, when refactoring, let's run our test and verify we did not break our tests. Our refactored tests yield the following results:

```
Run options:

# Running tests:

..

Finished tests in 44.988988s, 0.0445 tests/s, 0.1334 assertions/s.

2 tests, 6 assertions, 0 failures, 0 errors, 0 skips
```

Choosing the test environment

Now that the environment URL is hidden from the test, switching between the staging, test, and production environments will become easy. By using environment variables, we can control a lot of the test data at runtime.

 Environment variables are dynamically named values at the operating system level. Using the environment variables, the application behavior can be easily altered. To set an environment variable value, through the Command Line Interface on Windows, we run the following command:

```
set environment=staging
```

On UNIX-based systems, we use the `export` command to set environment variables, as follows:

```
export environment=production
```

Let's create a method our tests will use to retrieve the current test environment. Let's take a look at this method in the TestData class:

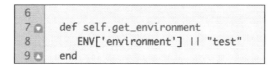

```
6
7   def self.get_environment
8       ENV['environment'] || "test"
9   end
```

The `get_environment` method uses the `ENV['environment']` call to see whether the `environment` variable is set on the current system. If it's not set, then our environment will default to `test`; this way we are never accidently testing in the production environment.

 Always have safety measures in place to prevent production testing with automated tests. Having a localhost or test environment is the best default value.

Next, let's update our `get_base_url` method to hold every test environment we have in a hash. As you can see in the following screenshot, the hash contains a key value pair of the environment name and URL it uses, and we use the `get_environment` method to choose the appropriate URL:

```
11  def self.get_base_url
12    {
13      "production" => "http://awful-valentine.com/",
14      "staging"   => "http://staging.awful-valentine.com/",
15      "test"      => "http://test.awful-valentine.com/"
16    }[self.get_environment]
17  end
```

Let's set the environment in the terminal and run our tests again to make sure everything is still passing. The following screenshot demonstrates the test run output; the underlined section shows us how to set a different environment:

```
mbp-3:code dima$ export environment=production
mbp-3:code dima$ ruby product_review_test.rb
Run options:

# Running tests:

..

Finished tests in 43.820089s, 0.0456 tests/s, 0.1369 assertions/s.

2 tests, 6 assertions, 0 failures, 0 errors, 0 skips
```

And that's it! Our tests can now run on three different environments, and all we have to do is specify the test environment we want our tests to run against. Now that the URL of the website is no longer hardcoded and can be dynamically specified at runtime, we can start migrating test data into fixtures.

> For the purpose of this book, our test, staging, and production environments are actually the same, but we will pretend that different web addresses go to a different environment.

Introducing test fixtures

In software development, test fixtures (fixtures) is a term used to describe any test data that lives outside of that particular test, and is used to set the application to a known fixed state. Fixtures allow us to have a constant to compare individual test runs against.

Fixtures work best in any environment that is high on the accessibility scale. If we are testing on the localhost or in the CI environment, we can start with a completely empty test database and fill it up with fixture data. When the tests are ready to run, the tests will know the exact state of the application, how many registered users we have, prices of every product, and so on. Let's take a look at a sample fixture, which was used to create a product on our website:

```
fixture_1:
  id: 1
  name: Closeness and Togetherness
  description: Show how much you appreciate just how close the two of you are
  rating: 0.5
  price: 5.77
  url: /closeness-and-togetherness
  image: /wp-content/uploads/2014/02/beeing_close_together.png
```

A script parsed the YAML fixture file and then inserted the YAML data into the website's database. As you can see, our fixtures are really simple and easy to read. This is a great advantage of using the YAML format for data, because it is easy for both humans and machines to read.

 YAML is an acronym for *YAML Ain't a Markup Language*. Unlike XML and **Comma Separated Value** (CSV) formats, YAML tries to display data in a matter that is as readable as possible.

Parsing fixture data

Parsing YAML fixtures in Ruby is surprisingly simple. After telling Ruby where the fixture file is, it will do a lot of work for us; the end result is a simple hash filled with data.

 Parsing YAML, or any other data representation, differs between different programming languages. Since the programming idioms vary so greatly between programming languages, follow the best standards for the toolset you have at hand.

Since the test fixture file is quite large, we will need to download it from `http://awful-valentine.com/code/chapter-4` and save it as `product_fixtures.yml` to continue our work. After the fixture file has been downloaded, let's modify the `test_data.rb` file to look like this:

```
1   require 'yaml'
2
3   class TestData
4     def self.get_product_fixtures
5       fixture_file = File.join(File.dirname(__FILE__), 'product_fixtures.yml')
6       YAML.load_file(fixture_file)
7     end
8
```

The `TestData` class has two modifications; the first one is an online one, where we required a YAML parsing library in our class. The second modification is the addition of the `get_product_fixtures` method, which reads the contents of `product_fixtures.yml` and returns the parsed file as a large hash.

Using fixture data in the tests

In *Chapter 3*, *Refactoring Tests*, we created the `select_desired_product_on_homepage` method to click on the **MORE INFO** button for a given product. The method looks like this:

```
def select_desired_product_on_homepage
  click('.special-item a[href*="our-love-is-special"].more-info')
end
```

As explained previously, this method chooses a product to review based on the HREF attribute of the **MORE INFO** button. When inspecting the fixture data, it is easy to find the permalink URL for every single product offered on the website. The permalink is a permanent static and unique link for any given page. Let's take a look at the permalink in fixtures:

```
27
28  fixture_4:
29    id: 4
30    name: Our love is special!!
31    description: Why do you stay together after years and years of fighting and childish behavior?
32    rating: 3.5
33    price: 68.99
34    url: /our-love-is-special
35    image: /wp-content/uploads/2014/02/more_than_meets_the_eye.png
36
```

Because the fixtures allow us to use the permalink of every product available, we no longer need to have the HREF attribute hardcoded. Let's modify the select_desired_product_on_homepage method to accept different permalinks such as the one shown in the following screenshot:

```
def select_desired_product_on_homepage(permalink)
    click(".special-item a[href*='#{permalink}'].more-info")
end
```

Now, let's update the setup method to get the product permalink from TestData, and store it as a @product_permalink instance variable, as follows:

```
7
8    def setup
9      @product_permalink = TestData.get_product_fixtures["fixture_4"]["url"]
10     @selenium = Selenium::WebDriver.for(:firefox)
11   end
12
```

The final change is to modify the generate_new_product_review method, so that it uses the @product_permalink variable, as seen here:

```
63
64   def generate_new_product_review(review)
65     navigate_to_homepage
66     select_desired_product_on_homepage(@product_permalink)
67     fill_out_comment_form(review)
68     get_newly_created_review_id
69   end
70
```

Once more, let's rerun our tests to make sure everything is still passing. The test results should look something like this:

```
# Running tests:

..

Finished tests in 53.800165s, 0.0372 tests/s, 0.1115 assertions/s.

2 tests, 6 assertions, 0 failures, 0 errors, 0 skips
```

Using fixtures to validate products

Before we started to refactor tests in *Chapter 3, Refactoring Tests*, our tests were working too much. Not only were they trying to create a new product review, but they were also trying to verify the information displayed on the page for a given product. We removed that assertion with a promise to create a test, whose only job would be to verify products. Now that we have access to the product fixtures, we can write a test for every product sold on our website. Let's create `product_validation_test.rb` to do just that. The contents of the file are as follows:

```
✗ product_validation_test.rb
1   require 'rubygems'
2   require 'selenium-webdriver'
3   require 'test/unit'
4   require File.join(File.dirname(__FILE__), 'test_data')
5
6   class ProductValidationTests < Test::Unit::TestCase
7     def setup
8       @selenium = Selenium::WebDriver.for(:firefox)
9     end
10
11    def teardown
12      @selenium.quit
13    end
14
15    def test_validate_our_love_is_special
16
17    end
18  end
19
```

So far, everything in our new file should look familiar to the previous tests we have written. Since we have the permalink for the product being tested, we do not need to land on the home page and click on the **MORE INFO** button for that product. Instead, we will have our test go directly to the product page.

> Since we navigate directly to the product's page, we are making our tests more resilient. Even if the home page of the website does not load properly, this test will be able to check individual products.

In the following code, we store the fixture for the tested product in the `product_info` variable and then combine it with `TestData.get_base_url` to navigate directly to the product's page:

```
14
15   def test_validate_our_love_is_special
16       product_info = TestData.get_product_fixtures["fixture_4"]
17       @selenium.get(TestData.get_base_url + product_info["url"])
18   end
```

Once the product pages load, we can start validating that everything was rendered correctly. Let's add four assertions to our test, shown as follows, and understand what each one does:

```
15   def test_validate_our_love_is_special
16       product_info = TestData.get_product_fixtures["fixture_4"]
17       @selenium.get(TestData.get_base_url + product_info["url"])
18
19       assert_equal(product_info["name"], @selenium.find_element(:class, "category-title").text)
20       assert_equal("#{TestData.get_base_url + product_info["url"]}/", @selenium.current_url)
21       assert_equal(product_info["description"], @selenium.find_element(:id, "main-products").find_element(:class, "content").text)
22       assert_equal(product_info["price"], @selenium.find_element(:class, "price-tag").text.gsub(/[\n\$]/, ""))
23   end
```

Our first assertion is on line **19**; we compare the product's name from fixtures against what is displayed in the DIV with the `category-title` class. On the next line, we compare the current URL of the product page against the URL generated from the fixtures. On line **21**, we verify the product description, followed by the product's price on line **22**.

> When comparing the product price, we used the `gsub` method to find and delete any instance of a new line character (\n) and the dollar sign ($).

Let's see the test result of our new test case:

```
mbp-3:code dima$ ruby product_validation_test.rb
Run options:
                              New Test File
# Running tests:

.

Finished tests in 5.628896s, 0.1777 tests/s, 0.7106 assertions/s.

1 tests, 4 assertions, 0 failures, 0 errors, 0 skips
```

Before we move on to the next section, let's refactor a little. Since searching for individual elements on the page may look too cryptic, let's move these out into methods, which are easy to understand. Our refactored code will look like this:

```
15  def test_validate_our_love_is_special
16    product_info = TestData.get_product_fixtures["fixture_4"]
17    @selenium.get(TestData.get_base_url + product_info["url"])
18
19    assert_equal(product_info["name"], get_product_title)
20    assert_equal("#{TestData.get_base_url + product_info["url"]}/", get_current_url)
21    assert_equal(product_info["description"], get_product_description)
22    assert_equal(product_info["price"], get_product_price)
23  end
24
25  private
26
27  def get_product_title
28    @selenium.find_element(:class, "category-title").text
29  end
30
31  def get_product_description
32    @selenium.find_element(:id, "main-products").find_element(:class, "content").text
33  end
34
35  def get_product_price
36    @selenium.find_element(:class, "price-tag").text.gsub(/[\n\$]/, "")
37  end
38
39  def get_current_url
40    @selenium.current_url
41  end
```

Is test refactoring becoming a habit yet? It should be! Our goal is to constantly improve the quality of our tests; even if it is something as simple as renaming a method so it better explains its actions.

 This refactoring might seem unnecessary at first, but six months from now when we are updating this test to accommodate new functionalities, will you remember what #main-products .content is?

Testing the remaining products

We are currently at a crossroad, and need to make a decision on how to proceed with adding tests for the remaining products. We can create a test for every single product or loop through the fixtures and programmatically test every product. Technically, there is no right or wrong choice here; both the options have advantages and disadvantages. When faced with a similar situation, we should weigh the pros and cons of each approach and select the right answer for the given moment. Let's compare multiple test models to the loop model.

Multiple test models

There are several advantages to writing a test for every single product in our store; let's take a look at some of them:

- **Clear test**: Each test clearly describes the product it is testing. At a glance, we can tell how many products we are testing and how long the test run will take.

- **Clear test failure**: When a test fails for any product, we will know right away which product it was by simply looking at the name of the test. A clear test failure should never be underestimated, especially if the test suite has 1,000 similar-looking tests.

- **Parallel execution**: When we have many individual tests, we can execute them all in parallel.

Since every coin has two sides, this approach has some disadvantages too. Let's take a look at those:

- **More verbose**: If we are only going to test a handful of products, this approach is perfectly good. However, if we were to test 30 products, our test file would grow in size rapidly.

- **Duplication**: Each test is identical to every other test; the only difference being the product it is testing. Managing these many tests can get tiresome quickly.

A single test model

Now that we weighed the advantages and disadvantages of the verbose option, let's take a look at the idea of having a single test that loops through the products. It has some very distinct advantages:

- **Less duplication**: This one is obvious; a single test is always cleaner than two dozen duplicates.

- **Automatic catalog updates**: If our product catalog changes in the future and we add or subtract some items in the fixture, our test will follow suit. There's no need to add or delete new tests at all, out of sight and out of mind!

- **Faster runtime**: Having a single test means that we will not have to restart our web browser every time a test is completed. These restarts will save a significant portion of the runtime compared to multiple tests.

 If we run our test suite in parallel, this argument becomes weaker.

However, there are some disadvantages to looping though all of the products:

- **Obfuscation**: Every time a new product is tested, there is no clear separation between the products. We will have to add some very clear messages to our tests to make sure that we can quickly find which product was not meeting our expectations.

- **Testing all the products**: The old proverb goes, "When you are a hammer, everything looks like a nail." Just because we can test every single product, should we really do it? Generally, if three or four of our products are rendered correctly, chances are the rest will be rendered in a similar fashion. Automatically testing every new product added can be a waste of resources; if we have to write a test for each product, we might get tired and stop adding new ones after the fifth or sixth test we write.

- **Single test runtime increase**: If our test is very involved, we can look at a 20-minute runtime to cover several products. This might not seem like a big problem at first, but let's pretend that we want to reduce the test execution time by running our tests in parallel. By running seven tests at the same time, we can reduce the suite runtime to 10 minutes, except for that one 20 minute test; our test suite is as fast as the slowest running test.

Implementing multiple test models

At some point, we all have to make a decision between having many tests that are easy to debug and having one complicated test. Make sure you do not rush into anything without considering the consequences of every approach. Since copying and pasting half a dozen new tests does not take much imagination, we will implement a single complicated test here.

Let's start by renaming `test_validate_our_love_is_special` to something a little more generic, such as `test_all_products_with_fixtures`. Next, we create a loop to go through all of the parsed fixtures; the loop looks like this:

```
TestData.get_product_fixtures.values.each
```

Now, every time the loop moves to the next product from the fixtures file, it will store the current fixture in the product_info variable (designated with an arrow). The refactored test now looks like this:

```
15   def test_all_products_with_fixtures
16     TestData.get_product_fixtures.values.each do | product_info |
17       @selenium.get(TestData.get_base_url + product_info["url"])
18
19       assert_equal(product_info["name"], get_product_title)
20       assert_equal("#{TestData.get_base_url + product_info["url"]}/", get_current_url)
21       assert_equal(product_info["description"], get_product_description)
22       assert_equal(product_info["price"], get_product_price)
23     end
24   end
```

After we run the new test, we will see right away that every single product page is now visited in the browser. Also, notice that the assertion count went up to 24:

```
# Running tests:

.

Finished tests in 15.001386s, 0.0667 tests/s, 1.5999 assertions/s.

1 tests, 24 assertions, 0 failures, 0 errors, 0 skips
```

Making test failures more expressive

Sadly, by using the looping approach, we gave up expressive test failures. If we had an individual test per product, we could look at the test name and instantly know which product failed. In the current state, test failures will look like this:

```
1) Failure:
test_all_products_with_fixtures(ProductValidationTests) [product_validation_test.rb:42]:
<"After \\n a long hard day at work, or with kids, you should not have a silly little fight about how y
y just how much your significant other cares about this day!"> expected but was
<"After a long hard day at work, or with kids, you should not have a silly little fight about how you f
st how much your significant other cares about this day!">.
```

Outside the very long string of text that shows the difference between expectation and reality, we have very little clue about the product that is not being rendered properly. We now have to open up the fixture file and find the description that will match our failure, so that we can understand why our test failed.

There is a way to make our tests more descriptive; we do this by passing a third parameter into the `assert_equals` method. The third parameter can be an arbitrary string that will be displayed on a failed assertion. Let's store some information about the product in the `failure_info` variable, like this:

```
failure_info = "Product Name: #{product_info['name']} \nPermalink #{product_info['url']}\n"
```

Our assertions now accept the `failure_info` parameter, and they look like this:

```
19        failure_info = "Product Name: #{product_info['name']} \nPermalink #{product_info['url']}\n"
20        assert_equal(product_info["name"], get_product_title, failure_info)
21        assert_equal("#{TestData.get_base_url + product_info["url"]}/", get_current_url, failure_info)
22        assert_equal(product_info["description"], get_product_description, failure_info)
23        assert_equal(product_info["price"], get_product_price, failure_info)
```

The result of this simple modification is that our test failures are a lot simpler to understand. Take a look at the new test failure message:

```
1) Failure:
test_all_products_with_fixtures(ProductValidationTests) [product_validation_test.rb:42]:
Product Name: Never Forget The Special Day!
Permalink /never-forget-the-special-day
.
<"After \\n a long hard day at work, or with kids, you should not have a silly little fight about how you
y just how much your significant other cares about this day!"> expected but was
<"After a long hard day at work, or with kids, you should not have a silly little fight about how you forg
st how much your significant other cares about this day!">.
```

The additional information in a test failure does not take a lot of effort to implement, which makes debugging failures so much simpler for everyone involved.

> Make sure your test provides too much information, because having too little information is always regrettable.

Using an API as a source of fixture data

Using fixtures for test data is great for environments that are highly accessible. If we need to test something other than the localhost or CI environment, where we cannot easily load fixture data into the database, we will have to use a different approach. The trick is to utilize any and all the resources we can find to make testing possible.

One of these resources is a public-facing web API. If your website has a native cell phone application or uses a lot of AJAX to load content, then our tests can have some data to test. All we have to do is interrogate the API to get an idea of the state of the application.

A common API endpoint for most e-commerce websites is a list of all the available products. This list is used by mobile phones to display what a user can purchase. Our website stores the product catalog at `http://api.awful-valentine.com/`; if you navigate to this URL in your browser, you will see something like this:

```
{
    "id": 1,
    "name": "Closeness and Togetherness",
    "description": "Show how much you appreciate just how close the two of you are",
    "rating": 0.5,
    "price": "5.77",
    "url": "closeness-and-togetherness",
    "image": "/wp-content/uploads/2014/02/beeing_close_together.png"
},
```

Our API endpoint returns a product catalog in the **JavaScript Object Notation (JSON)** format. If we compare our test fixtures to the returned JSON, we will find a lot of similarities; in fact, the data is identical! By consuming the product catalog, we are able to create a similar test we just made. Let's begin by adding two more libraries to the `test_data.rb` file, shown here:

```
× test_data.rb
1   require 'yaml'
2   require 'net/http'
3   require 'json'
4
```

We will be using these libraries to make an HTTP request against the website's API endpoint. Then, we will use the `json` library to parse the received data and use it in the test. Now we are going to add a method to the `TestData` class called `get_products_from_api`. It looks like this:

```
10
11   def self.get_products_from_api
12     uri = URI.parse("http://api.awful-valentine.com")
13     json_string = Net::HTTP.get(uri)
14     JSON.parse(json_string)
15   end
16
```

Let's take a look at individual things happening in this method. On line **12**, we create a `URI` object from a string. We pass this object to the `Net::HTTP.get` method call on line **13** and get a string of unparsed JSON in return. Finally, use the `JSON.parse` method to parse the string and return the value as a hash. We have a way to get the product catalog from the environment; let's create a test to take advantage of this data.

We will add a new test called `test_all_products_with_api_response` and it will be 98 percent identical to `test_all_products_with_fixtures`. Let's take a look at both the tests side by side, with the major differences pointed out:

```
14
15   def test_all_products_with_fixtures
16     TestData.get_product_fixtures.values.each do | product_info |
17       @selenium.get(TestData.get_base_url + product_info["url"])
18
19       failure_info = "Product Name: #{product_info['name']} \nPermalink #{product_info['url']}\n"
20       assert_equal(product_info["name"], get_product_title, failure_info)
21       assert_equal("#{TestData.get_base_url + product_info["url"]}/", get_current_url, failure_info)
22       assert_equal(product_info["description"], get_product_description, failure_info)
23       assert_equal(product_info["price"], get_product_price, failure_info)
24     end
25   end
26
27   def test_all_products_with_api_response
28     TestData.get_products_from_api.each do |product_info|
29       @selenium.get(TestData.get_base_url + product_info["url"])
30
31       failure_info = "Product Name: #{product_info['name']} \nPermalink #{product_info['url']}\n"
32       assert_equal(product_info["name"], get_product_title, failure_info)
33       assert_equal("#{TestData.get_base_url + product_info["url"].gsub(/^\//, "")}/", get_current_url, failure_info)
34       assert_equal(product_info["description"], get_product_description, failure_info)
35       assert_equal(product_info["price"].to_s, get_product_price, failure_info)
36     end
37   end
38
```

Let's save and run both the tests. Our test results should now look like this:

```
# Running tests:

. .

Finished tests in 25.316024s, 0.0790 tests/s, 1.8960 assertions/s.

2 tests, 48 assertions, 0 failures, 0 errors, 0 skips
```

As always, when we get our tests running, it's time to refactor the duplication. Let's take a look at the final product; all of it should look familiar and make sense:

```
14
15   def test_all_products_with_fixtures
16     TestData.get_product_fixtures.values.each do | product_info |
17       @selenium.get(TestData.get_base_url + product_info["url"])
18       verify_product_info(product_info)
19     end
20   end
21
22   def test_all_products_with_api_response
23     TestData.get_products_from_api.each do |product_info|
24       @selenium.get(TestData.get_base_url + product_info["url"])
25       verify_product_info(product_info)
26     end
27   end
28
29   private
30
31   def verify_product_info(product_info)
32     failure_info = "Product Name: #{product_info['name']} \nPermalink #{product_info['url']}\n"
33     assert_equal(product_info["name"], get_product_title, failure_info)
34     assert_equal("#{TestData.get_base_url + product_info["url"].gsub(/^\//, "")}/", get_current_url, failure_info)
35     assert_equal(product_info["description"], get_product_description, failure_info)
36     assert_equal(product_info["price"].to_s, get_product_price, failure_info)
37   end
38
```

Using data stubs

Modern websites are incredibly complicated and combine many external services. Most e-commerce websites do not actually process the credit cards themselves. Instead, the payment information is passed on to the bank, and the bank tells the website whether the transaction is successful.

Getting all of the external services running is a difficult task, especially if the service our website is using is also being developed at the same time as our project. We cannot afford to wait until all of the services are completely written and integrated to start writing our tests. So, we have to stub some of the services until they are fully developed.

Stubs are premade responses to our application's requests. Stub responses are formatted and look like real responses, but they don't actually do any work. For example, the API endpoint we used to write our test does not actually communicate with the database. Instead, it responds with a premade JSON file. Stubbing the application is a great way to set up a test environment for automated tests, and should be used as much as possible when running automated tests in the CI system.

The default values pattern

Filling out form information is one of the core principles of writing tests with Selenium. The test will need to register a new user, or make a purchase, or log in to an account at some point. The default values pattern aims to extract any data that our test does not actually care about. Tests should not have to know what the username and password are for every test user on every environment we have. Instead, it should rely on defaults that are appropriate for the current state.

Advantages of the default values pattern

Isolating irrelevant data from the test implementation has many advantages:

- **Need to know basis**: If our test is testing whether a purchase can be made with a credit card, the test does not need to know which credit card was used. However, if our test needs to check whether a certain credit card is accepted, then the card number is known to the test.

- **Simpler tests**: Extracting all of the unnecessary data out of the test implementation makes the test easier to read and understand.

- **More focus**: While writing the test, it is easy to get distracted with data that is used in the test setup. Having all of the setup data handed to us as we are writing the test, allows us to concentrate on the test implementation.

- **Overwrite only important values**: If we are testing the registration flow, we only care that the username is unique. The default values pattern allows you to provide just the important values while reusing the defaults.

Disadvantages of the default values pattern

There aren't many disadvantages to the default values pattern, but here are the top two:

- **Implementing overwrite**: Depending on the programming language and framework used to write the test, we might need to implement the data merge/overwrite logic ourselves.

- **Homogeneous data**: Having static default data might not always be preferable. In the comment-creation test, we had to add timestamps to the comment string to make the website accept our new comments. Using a library like **faker** can alleviate this pain point.

Merging the default values pattern and the faker library

Every test should strive to use input data that is as close to real life scenarios as possible. If our test always uses `test_selenium_user_34256` as the user's first and last name, we are not using our application in the same manner as our customers. For example, how will our application handle having a title in the name such as Mr., Sr., or PhD?

Faker is a library that was written to solve these types of scenarios. It has been ported into many programming languages including Perl, Java, and Ruby. For the rest of this chapter, we will implement the default values pattern and integrate the faker library into our test to help us create default values that mimic real world scenarios.

Implementing faker methods

Let's install the faker gem and implement several methods that will be used for the new comment form functionalities. We need to install the faker gem, since it is not shipped with Ruby; run the following command in your terminal:

```
gem install faker
```

Now, we are ready to modify the `test_data.rb` file. As always, we will require a faker library at the top of the file. Then, add a couple of methods to get some life-like data for our tests. The code for the `TestData` class, with additions annotated, looks like this:

```
1   require 'yaml'
2   require 'net/http'
3   require 'json'
4   require 'faker'          ◄──────────
5
6   class TestData
7
8       def self.get_full_name       ◄──────────
9           Faker::Name.name
10      end
11
12      def self.get_email
13          Faker::Internet.email    ◄──────────
14      end
15
16      def self.get_website
17          Faker::Internet.url      ◄──────────
18      end
19
20      def self.get_buzzword
21          Faker::Company.catch_phrase    ◄──────────
22      end
23
```

All of these faker methods should be self-explanatory, except for `get_buzzword`. This method is used to generate a catchphrase that some fortune 500 companies would use in their advertisements. Since these phrases are a collection of randomly pieced buzzwords, they will most likely be unique enough to be used in the comment section of our reviews. Let's create a method that ties all of these items together for us; we will call it `get_comment_form_values` and it will look like this:

```
23
24      def self.get_comment_form_values(overwrites = {})
25          {
26              :name    => self.get_full_name,
27              :email   => self.get_email,
28              :url     => self.get_website,
29              :comment => self.get_buzzword
30          }.merge(overwrites)
31      end
32
```

This method is not very complicated; all it does is create a new hash and then populates it with faker data. Here are a couple of key parts:

- This method accepts an optional parameter, `overwrites`, which defaults to an empty hash. This will allow us to overwrite any field value at will. Also, if we are so inclined, we can add a new key and value that is not set by this method. This makes the `get_comment_form_values` method incredibly flexible.

- After the hash with new fake data is created, we overwrite the generated values with values from `overwrites` by using the `merge(overwrites)` method.

Every time the `get_comment_form_values` method is executed, it will create beautifully nonsensical but real-world looking data. If we are to invoke this method in `irb`, we will get this output:

```
(rdb:1) pp TestData.get_comment_form_values
{:name=>"Kylee Reinger",
 :email=>"loyce.hills@shanahan.com",
 :url=>"http://greenfelderleannon.net/toni",
 :comment=>"Robust systematic encryption"}
```

The pp method call before the `TestData.get_comment_form_values` call is Ruby shorthand for Pretty Print. This allows us to see each value of the hash on a new line instead of a single long string.

Updating the comment test to use default values

We need to revisit `product_review_test.rb` to take advantage of the default values we just implemented in the `TestData` class. The implementation is actually quite simple and fast. Let's make it happen!

Remember the `fill_out_comment_form` method, which we wrote to fill out the review form? It looked like this the last time we modified it:

```
70
71   def fill_out_comment_form(comment)
72       type_text("Dima", "author", :id)
73       type_text("dima@@selenium.com", "email", :id)
74       type_text("http://awful-valentine.com", "url", :id)
75       click("a[title='5']")
76       find_element("comment", :id).clear
77       type_text(comment, "comment", :id)
78       click("submit", :id)
79   end
80
```

As we can see, most of the data it fills out is hardcoded, and only the portion that is not hardcoded is the comment variable. Our goal is to pass in every piece of data this method uses. We will rename the comment argument to form_info, to make our intentions more clear. This new argument is a hash, so we will have to retrieve the appropriate key for each field we fill out in the form. Let's take a look at the new code with the changes highlighted:

```
70
71    def fill_out_comment_form(form_info)
72        type_text(form_info[:name], "author", :id)
73        type_text(form_info[:email], "email", :id)
74        type_text(form_info[:url], "url", :id)
75        click("a[title='5']")
76        find_element("comment", :id).clear
77        type_text(form_info[:comment], "comment", :id)
78        click("submit", :id)
79    end
80
```

Let's modify test_add_new_review to use the faker methods. Our test, with changes highlighted, will now look like this:

```
18
19    def test_add_new_review
20      review_form_info = TestData.get_comment_form_values({:name => "Dima"})
21      review_id = generate_new_product_review(review_form_info)
22
23      review = @selenium.find_element(:id, review_id)
24
25      name = review.find_element(:class, "comment-author-metainfo").find_element(:class, "url").text
26      comment = review.find_element(:class, "comment-content").text
27
28      assert_equal("Dima", name)
29      assert_equal(review_form_info[:comment], comment)
30
31      parsed_date = DateTime.parse(review.find_element(:class, "comment-author-metainfo").find_element(:class, "commentmetadata").text)
32      assert_equal(Date.today.year, parsed_date.year)
33      assert_equal(Date.today.month, parsed_date.month)
34      assert_equal(Date.today.day, parsed_date.day)
35    end
36
```

The only major change in our test is on line **20**, where we no longer use the generate_unique_comment method, calling TestData.get_comment_form_values instead. Note that we are overwriting the faker value for :name with Dima to demonstrate the overwriting capability of our new method.

Finally, let's update `test_adding_a_duplicate_review` in a similar fashion so that it looks like this:

```
36
37    def test_adding_a_duplicate_review
38      review_form_info = TestData.get_comment_form_values
39      generate_new_product_review(review_form_info)
40      sleep 10
41      generate_new_product_review(review_form_info)
42
43      error = @selenium.find_element(:id, "error-page").text
44      assert_equal("Duplicate comment detected; it looks as though you\u2019ve already said that!", error)
45    end
46
```

And this wraps up the changes that we needed to finish. Let's run our tests to make sure everything still passes.

> Since we are no longer using the `generate_unique_comment` method in our tests, this is probably a good time to clean up our code base by deleting this and any other unused methods.

The test output should look like this:

```
Run options:

# Running tests:

. .

Finished tests in 45.917384s, 0.0436 tests/s, 0.1307 assertions/s.

2 tests, 6 assertions, 0 failures, 0 errors, 0 skips
```

Summary

To be completely honest, managing test data is by far the single most difficult task with test automation. Locating an element on a complicated web page pales in comparison in complexity, compared to dealing with test data. There are so many technical and legal restrictions whenever production data is used that maintaining a grid of hundreds of browsers will feel like a vacation.

In this chapter, we only scratched the surface of data management. By using fixtures, we can control some of the chaos in the CI test environment. When fixtures are not an option, we can find other ways to interrogate the state of the application by using API endpoints, or we can stub out external services to make sure our application can still function. With the use of the faker library and default values pattern, we can simplify our test implementation by generating real-looking data that has been abstracted away.

In the next chapter, we will be improving the stability of our small test suite. We will fix a lot of the common causes of instability, thereby making our test suite as stable as humanly possible.

5

Stabilizing the Tests

"And the rain descended, and the floods came, and the winds blew, and beat upon that house; and it fell not: for it was founded upon a rock."

-Matthew 7:25, King James Version

When the test suite becomes large enough, our job becomes less about the fixing every flaky test. In fact, it centers on engineering a solution that will prevent all similar flaky behavior from happening.

In this chapter, we will give our tests a good solid foundation that will prevent a lot of instability in the long run. We waited until this chapter to start fixing the behavior that drives anyone who writes web tests insane, because we had to first build up a foundation of good data management and coding skills. These skills are crucial for long-term use and without them, all of the fixes of instability discussed in this chapter would be useless. Now we're ready to talk about the following topics:

- Culture of stability
- jQuery
- Waiting for AJAX requests to finish
- Waiting for jQuery animations to finish
- The Action Wrapper pattern
- The Black Hole Proxy pattern
- Screenshot on failure practice

Engineering the culture of stability

I'd like to start the current chapter with a personal tale of a past experience. The majority of projects that I worked on had similar situation to what you are probably used to. Typically, the Selenium build is treated as a second-class citizen, not having a single passing build for days or weeks at the time. Eventually, the tests become so embarrassingly riddled with failures and instabilities that any further development is stopped, and the Selenium build is completely ignored.

On my last project I inherited 300 Selenium tests, which were red 90 percent of the time. So, I started to fix them but that was not enough; no sooner that I would fix a broken test, somebody would make a commit that broke another test somewhere else. I did not have a technical problem, I had a cultural problem; nobody but me seemed to care about Selenium tests.

The team that I was a part of was given the task of maintaining builds; with a lot of trial and error, we came up with several key goals that would lead all of our builds to be passing 99 percent of the time (less actual failures due to bad code). Here are the key goals, as I see them, for any CI system:

- Running fast and failing fast
- Running as often as possible
- Keeping a clean and consistent environment
- Discarding bad code changes
- Maintaining a stable test suite

Running fast and failing fast

A developer's time is very expensive. We cannot afford to let them sit around for 40 minutes to see whether all of the tests are passing after every minor code change. The goal is to run the whole test suite under 10 minutes, or the developer will not have an incentive to run the tests at all. Doing the simple math of the man hours spent by each developer on daily basis waiting for the build, compared to doing actual work, we had a very convincing argument to purchase a lot more test nodes for CI. With these new computers, we were able to run the test suite in parallel across multiple computers, bringing the whole build down to 12 minutes. Furthermore, we added some code to send an e-mail to the developer as soon as a test failed. This allows the developers to start fixing a broken test even before the build is complete.

Running as often as possible

Creating a cascading build chain, starting with unit tests and finishing with Selenium, is a common practice. However, this practice turned out to be an *anti-pattern*, a term discussed in *Chapter 2, The Spaghetti Pattern*. A typical Selenium build is the slowest in the series; thus, it occupies the last place where everyone can easily ignore it. Often, a failure early in the chain will prevent the Selenium build from ever being executed. By the time the long forgotten Selenium build is finally executed, a dozen code commits have occurred. Making sure that the Selenium build is triggered on every single commit seems excessive, but the whole idea of CI is to catch a test failure as soon as it occurs, not 20 changes down the road. Taking this idea to its logical conclusion, a code change should always be considered bad if even a single test fails.

Having the whole code base being deployed and tested with every code change also has an advantage of testing the deploy scripts continuously.

Keeping a clean and consistent environment

Unlike instability caused by test implementation, instability caused by inconsistent testing nodes can be more frustrating and harder to track down. Having different versions of Firefox or Internet Explorer on every test node might not seem like a big deal, but when a test fails because of such minor differences and the failure cannot be easily replicated, a lot of frustration will be experienced.

We discussed test fixtures in *Chapter 4, Data-driven Testing*; reloading the test database for every build is a great way to keep a clean and consistent test environment. Also, using a configuration management tool to keep all of the dependencies, such as Java versions, consistent on all of the test nodes will save you a lot of headaches. Finally, make sure that the test environment that serves your website is as close of a physical clone of production as you can make it. All of your tests can be completely invalid if your production uses Linux servers to host the website, but your test environment is hosted on a Windows computer.

There are several open source, free tools for the configuration management of computers. Two of the more popular ones are Chef (http://www.getchef.com/) and Puppet (http://puppetlabs.com/).

Discarding bad code changes

We set up a simple system that prevented anybody from committing changes to the master/trunk unless all of the tests, including Selenium, were passing. Needless to say, this was not a popular approach because tests from unrelated parts of the application were sometimes preventing new features from going into **Version Control System (VCS)**. However, as the test suite stabilized, this became a great way to prevent unintended defects from going into production, and making sure that the whole test suite, including Selenium, was always passing!

There are multiple ways to implement this, since most VCS systems allow users to define precommit or postcommit hooks. The other approach is to prevent direct commits to the trunk/master branches, instead deferring to a build that automatically merges the changes after all tests pass. The latter approach works best in GIT and Mercurial VCS tools.

Maintaining a stable test suite

Cultural changes will never last if your tests will fail at random due to technical problems such as not dealing with **AJAX** properly or not accounting for external influences that will make the test environment run slow. In this chapter, we will concentrate on some of the most common technical solutions that make tests unstable. Let's get going!

Asynchronous JavaScript and XML (AJAX) is a relatively new web development technique that allows the web page to send and receive content in the background.

Waiting for AJAX

Test automation was simpler in the good old days, before asynchronous page loading became mainstream. Previously, the test would click on a button causing the whole page to reload; after the new page loaded, we could check whether any errors were displayed. The act of waiting for the page to load guaranteed that all of the items on the page are already there, and our test could fail with confidence if the expected element was missing. Now, an element might be missing for several seconds, and magically show up after an unspecified delay. The only thing for a test to do is become smarter!

Filling out credit card information is a common test for any online store. Similarly, we set up a simple credit card purchase form that looks like this:

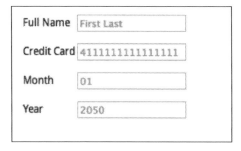

Our form has some default values for users to fill out and a quick JavaScript check to see whether the required information was entered into the field (by adding a quick **Done** text):

Once all of the fields have been filled out and seem correct, JavaScript makes the **Purchase** button clickable. Clicking on the button will trigger an AJAX request for the purchase, followed by successful purchase message:

The preceding steps were very simple and straightforward; anyone who has made an online purchase has seen some variation of this form. Writing a quick test to fill out the form and making sure the purchase is complete should be a breeze!

Testing without AJAX delays

Let's get started then. We have to add two new methods to the TestData class. We need one method to generate realistic credit card numbers and another method that generates expiration dates. These two new methods will look like this in the test_data.rb file:

```
 5
 6  class TestData
 7
 8    def self.get_credit_card_number
 9      Faker::Business.credit_card_number
10    end
11
12    def self.get_credit_card_expiry_date
13      Faker::Business.credit_card_expiry_date
14    end
15
```

Faker is really good at generating test credit cards that will pass the Luhn test. This allows us to write tests against purchase forms that have simple JavaScript validation for the validity of the card number.

> The Luhn test algorithm is a simple checksum formula created by Hans Peter Luhn. It is used by majority of credit card companies when generating an account number. Here are examples of a Luhn valid test credit cards for VISA: 4444 3333 2222 1111 and 4111 1111 1111 1111. Similarly, test numbers for MasterCard are 5555555555554444 and 5454545454545454.

Now let's create a new test file called purchase_form_test.rb. Let's take a look at our very simple PurchaseFormTests class; we will start with the same boilerplate code that we have seen many times in previous chapters:

```
✱ purchase_form_test.rb
1    require 'rubygems'
2    require 'selenium-webdriver'
3    require 'test/unit'
4    require File.join(File.dirname(__FILE__), 'test_data')
5    I18n.enforce_available_locales = false
6
7    class PurchaseFormTests < Test::Unit::TestCase
8
9      def setup
10       @selenium = Selenium::WebDriver.for(:firefox)
11     end
12
13     def teardown
14       @selenium.quit
15     end
16
```

Looking at the actual test, we should see a lot of similarities to the code we wrote in *Chapter 4, Data-driven Testing*. Let's take a quick look:

```
16
17   def test_fillout_purchase_form
18     @selenium.get(TestData.get_base_url + "/purchase-forms/perfect-world")
19
20     type_text(TestData.get_full_name, "name", :id)
21     type_text(TestData.get_credit_card_number, "cc", :id)
22     type_text(TestData.get_credit_card_expiry_date.month, "month", :id)
23     type_text(TestData.get_credit_card_expiry_date.year, "year", :id)
24
25     click("go", :id)
26
27     assert_equal("Purchase complete!", get_inner_text("success", :id))
28   end
29
```

We close the test file with the helper images in the `private` section:

```
29
30      private
31
32    def find_element(element, strategy=:css)
33        @selenium.find_element(strategy, element)
34    end
35
36    def type_text(text, element, strategy=:css)
37        find_element(element, strategy).send_keys(text)
38    end
39
40    def click(element, strategy=:css)
41        find_element(element, strategy).click
42    end
43
44    def get_inner_text(element, strategy=:css)
45        find_element(element, strategy).text
46    end
47  end
```

If we compare the code from this test with `product_review_test.rb` from the previous chapter, we will notice that the helper methods are pretty much identical. This is typically a good sign that a code refactors in order. However, before we can start refactoring, we should first concentrate on making the tests work.

 Remember, premature optimization is the root of all evil in software programming.

So, without any further delays, let's run our tests. Our output should look like this:

```
Run options:

# Running tests:

.

Finished tests in 4.946432s, 0.2022 tests/s, 0.2022 assertions/s.

1 tests, 1 assertions, 0 failures, 0 errors, 0 skips
```

We have a passing test for the purchase form; in a perfect world, our work would be complete. In the next section, let's take a look at a scenario that is a little more realistic.

Using explicit delays to test AJAX forms

We now have a test that will work perfectly well when testing the website against a fast test environment like localhost. These environments tend to *stub* the purchase form responses to create an environment that is easily testable in CI. However, our staging and production environments communicate with a third-party service to validate the credit card information.

 For more information about stubbing third-party services, visit *Chapter 4, Data-driven Testing*.

Let's see how well our tests do in such an environment. In the previous chapter, we implemented a concept of environment in the `TestData` class. It's time to put it to use by pointing our tests toward the staging environment with the help of command line variables. On a Windows-based computer, type the following command in the terminal:

```
set environment=staging
```

If you are using a Linux-based computer, including OS X, we will use the export command:

```
export environment="staging"
```

Now let's run our test the same way we just did. The terminal should now display this:

```
mbp-3:code dima$ export environment="staging"          Linux based export command
mbp-3:code dima$ ruby purchase_form_test.rb
Run options:

# Running tests:

F

Finished tests in 12.356959s, 0.0809 tests/s, 0.0809 assertions/s.

  1) Failure:                                            Test failure
test_fillout_purchase_form(PurchaseFormTests) [purchase_form_test.rb:27]:
<"Purchase complete!"> expected but was
<"">.

1 tests, 1 assertions, 1 failures, 0 errors, 0 skips
```

What went wrong? If we were watching the test run on the monitor, we would notice that the **Purchase complete!** message did not appear instantly. Instead, we saw an AJAX request indicator, colloquially known as spinner, as shown in the following screenshot:

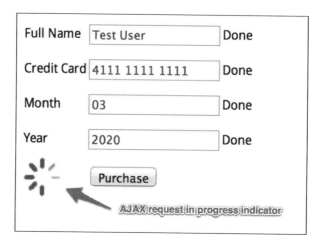

Since the `success` DIV only shows the **Purchase complete!** text after the asynchronous request is completed, our test only saw an empty string; thus it failed. The most obvious and fastest way to fix our test is to add a `sleep` command to allow the AJAX request to complete. The code will look like this:

```
16
17  def test_fillout_purchase_form
18    @selenium.get(TestData.get_base_url + "/purchase-forms/perfect-world")
19
20    type_text(TestData.get_full_name, "name", :id)
21    type_text(TestData.get_credit_card_number, "cc", :id)
22    type_text(TestData.get_credit_card_expiry_date.month, "month", :id)
23    type_text(TestData.get_credit_card_expiry_date.year, "year", :id)
24
25    click("go", :id)
26    sleep 25 ◀━━━━━━━━━━━
27    assert_equal("Purchase complete!", get_inner_text("success", :id))
28  end
29
```

Just like every other anti-pattern, this quick fix makes our tests pass right away with some long term unintended consequences. In this particular case, the purchase form's AJAX request will take up to 30 seconds to complete. Telling the test to pause for 25 seconds raises these issues:

- **Wasted time**: The majority of the requests made by the purchase form will finish in less than 15 seconds. This means that our tests will be doing nothing even though the page is in ready state.

 Avoiding unnecessary delays becomes very important as the test suite grows. Remember, we want the whole test suite to finish in 10 minutes or less.

- **Environment unaware**: Only the staging environment has such a delay with the AJAX request, the CI environment gives an instant response. As mentioned in previous point, this is wasted time.

- **Wait can be too short**: Once in a while the staging environment or the third-party service can be under heavy load and the request might take longer than 30 seconds. The hardcoded sleep value is not adequate enough to deal with real-world scenarios.

What we need is to make our tests smart enough to know when the AJAX request to complete.

Implementing intelligent delays

There are a lot of JavaScript frameworks that allow developers to implement asynchronous request functionality with ease. One of the most popular is called **jQuery**, which implements a lot of useful functionality outside AJAX requests. One of the API calls that jQuery provides is ability to get the total current count of active asynchronous requests. Executing `jQuery.active` function call from JavaScript will return `0` if the page is fully loaded and it will return a nonzero number if there are current background requests.

Selenium WebDriver allows our tests to execute arbitrary JavaScript commands within the context of the current web page with `execute_script` method. If we combine all of these items together in a `wait_for_ajax` method, we can make our tests treat background requests intelligently.

If your current project does not use jQuery to make AJAX requests, check the documentation of your framework for something analogous to `jQuery.active`. If all else fails, you can take Dave Haeffner's approach of injecting jQuery into a web page that does not have it included. You can find his blog post at `http://elementalselenium.com/tips/53-growl`.

Let's take a look at the `wait_for_ajax` method implementation:

```
47
48   def wait_for_ajax
49     Selenium::WebDriver::Wait.new(:timeout => 60).until do
50       sleep 1
51       @selenium.execute_script("return jQuery.active") == 0
52     end
53   end
54
```

There is a lot going on here; so let's break things down a little starting on line **49**. We create a new instance of the `Wait` class provided by Selenium WebDriver. When creating this new class, we explicitly set the timeout to be 60 seconds; when the timeout is reached, the test will get back the control and move to the next step. The `Wait` class has an `until` method that accepts a block of code, line **50** and **51**.

In WebDriver, the `until` method in the `Wait` class is simply a loop that executes the contents of the code block passed to it until the code returns a `true` value. In the case of the `wait_for_ajax` method, the exit loop condition is reached when there are 0 active AJAX requests. We ask the JavaScript to `return jQuery.active` count. Finally, we compare the returned integer value to `0`. If the conditional returns `true`, all of AJAX requests finished and we are ready to move to the next step.

Now, we just add the `wait_for_ajax` invocation anywhere we need our tests to wait. We will be replacing the hardcoded sleep method from earlier, as shown here:

```
24
25     click("go", :id)
26     wait_for_ajax
27     assert_equal("Purchase complete!", get_inner_text("success", :id))
```

As a good habit, after we refactor any code, we run our tests to make sure everything is passing. Let's take a look at the test results with the `wait_for_ajax` method included. In the following screenshot, we can see that the total execution time of the test went up to accommodate the background AJAX request:

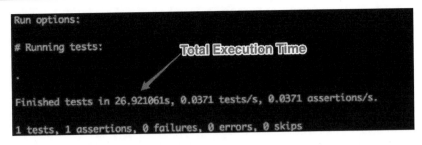

We conquered the AJAX menace. It's time to move on to the next cause of instability on modern websites: JavaScript animations.

Waiting for JavaScript animations

When websites started to use AJAX, the developers and designers faced a new challenge. Previously, any major interaction with a website, such as clicking the purchase button, gave a user clear indication that something is changing after each action. With asynchronous requests, parts of the web page can change and user would not notice that something important has happened. So, the designers came up with ways to draw user's attention towards the section of the page that has changed. It started with fading in the changing content in a yellow box, slowly incorporated a spiny wheel, and now we have whole page swipes and many other animations to accomplish this.

 Animation is an act of changing the web page; it ranges from adding or subtracting images to removing everything on the page and starting over.

There are several situations in which a Selenium test will fail with `ElementNotVisibleError` even though the element we are looking for is technically on the page. If our test is attempting to click on a button, the following conditions will prevent the click:

- **Not currently visible**: Some websites place the button somewhere on the page, but make it invisible until it is ready to be clicked. Often, they will use an animated transition effect to slowly fade in the button to make the experience feel pleasant. Attempting to click on the element, which is still transparent, will not be successful.

- **Under other elements**: Let's say a defect is introduced in the page layout where some element such as a text input is out of place and ends up covering up the button we wish to click on. The button is present on the screen and technically functional. However, since the human user is not able to point the mouse at it and click it, WebDriver will not allow the test to click on it either.

- **Offscreen**: A common design practice is adding elements to the page but placing them far offscreen, and using JavaScript to slide them into view when certain conditions are met. The transition enhances the user's experience. Attempting to click on an element that has not yet slid into place will make WebDriver throw `ElementNotVisibleError`.

Test failures caused by element animation are some of the most difficult to debug. Even if we take a screenshot of the entire page at the point of failure, the element finished rendering. This leads to a situation where the test claims that an element is missing, but the screenshot shows that element in fact is present. In other words, making our tests wait for AJAX requests to complete is not enough; they also need to wait for JavaScript animations to finish. To demonstrate a test failure due to JavaScript animation, let's modify the target URL of our test to this:

```
16
17    def test_fillout_purchase_form
18        @selenium.get(TestData.get_base_url + "/purchase-forms/slow-animation")
19
20        type_text(TestData.get_full_name, "name", :id)
```

This page contains a purchase form similar to the ones we have been dealing with, with one minor difference. The **Purchase** button is invisible until enough text fields are filled out; after a threshold for completeness is reached, the **Purchase** button slowly fades in. The following screenshot shows the purchase form before the animation complete and after the animation is complete:

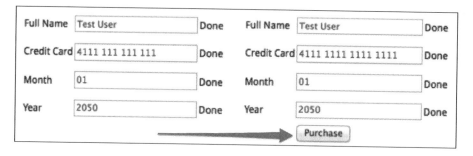

If we run our test without any modifications, we will get the following test failure in our output:

```
1) Error:
test_fillout_purchase_form(PurchaseFormTests):
Selenium::WebDriver::Error::ElementNotVisibleError: Element is not currently visible and so may not be interacted with
    [remote server] file:///var/folders/r6/vlz_ftgx6xz36xdz6tfl31lw0000gp/T/webdriver-profile20140814-10200-fk1mml/extensions/fxdriver@googlecode.com
    [remote server] file:///var/folders/r6/vlz_ftgx6xz36xdz6tfl31lw0000gp/T/webdriver-profile20140814-10200-fk1mml/extensions/fxdriver@googlecode.com
    [remote server] file:///var/folders/r6/vlz_ftgx6xz36xdz6tfl31lw0000gp/T/webdriver-profile20140814-10200-fk1mml/extensions/fxdriver@googlecode.com
    [remote server] file:///var/folders/r6/vlz_ftgx6xz36xdz6tfl31lw0000gp/T/webdriver-profile20140814-10200-fk1mml/extensions/fxdriver@googlecode.com
    [remote server] file:///var/folders/r6/vlz_ftgx6xz36xdz6tfl31lw0000gp/T/webdriver-profile20140814-10200-fk1mml/extensions/fxdriver@googlecode.com
/Users/dima/.rvm/gems/ruby-1.9.3-p362@book/gems/selenium-webdriver-2.42.0/lib/selenium/webdriver/remote/response.rb:51:in `assert_ok'
/Users/dima/.rvm/gems/ruby-1.9.3-p362@book/gems/selenium-webdriver-2.42.0/lib/selenium/webdriver/remote/response.rb:15:in `initialize'
/Users/dima/.rvm/gems/ruby-1.9.3-p362@book/gems/selenium-webdriver-2.42.0/lib/selenium/webdriver/remote/http/common.rb:59:in `new'
/Users/dima/.rvm/gems/ruby-1.9.3-p362@book/gems/selenium-webdriver-2.42.0/lib/selenium/webdriver/remote/http/common.rb:59:in `create_response'
/Users/dima/.rvm/gems/ruby-1.9.3-p362@book/gems/selenium-webdriver-2.42.0/lib/selenium/webdriver/remote/http/default.rb:66:in `request'
/Users/dima/.rvm/gems/ruby-1.9.3-p362@book/gems/selenium-webdriver-2.42.0/lib/selenium/webdriver/remote/http/common.rb:40:in `call'
/Users/dima/.rvm/gems/ruby-1.9.3-p362@book/gems/selenium-webdriver-2.42.0/lib/selenium/webdriver/remote/bridge.rb:634:in `raw_execute'
/Users/dima/.rvm/gems/ruby-1.9.3-p362@book/gems/selenium-webdriver-2.42.0/lib/selenium/webdriver/remote/bridge.rb:612:in `execute'
/Users/dima/.rvm/gems/ruby-1.9.3-p362@book/gems/selenium-webdriver-2.42.0/lib/selenium/webdriver/remote/bridge.rb:369:in `clickElement'
/Users/dima/.rvm/gems/ruby-1.9.3-p362@book/gems/selenium-webdriver-2.42.0/lib/selenium/webdriver/common/element.rb:54:in `click'
purchase_form_test.rb:41:in `click'
purchase_form_test.rb:25:in `test_fillout_purchase_form'
```

To fix this problem, we will need to create a `wait_for_animation` method, which similarly to the `wait_for_ajax` method from earlier, will be intelligent enough to allow JavaScript to finish its tasks. Let's take a look at this method:

```
55
56  def wait_for_animation
57    Selenium::WebDriver::Wait.new(:timeout => 60).until do
58      sleep 1
59      @selenium.execute_script("return jQuery(':animated').length") == 0
60    end
61  end
62
```

This method looks identical to the `wait_for_ajax` method. The only difference is the JavaScript command passed into `execute_script` method. We use the `jQuery(':animated').length` command to find how many animations are currently in progress; when total animation count hits 0, we move on to the next step in our test. Let's add this method to our tests as shown here:

```
24
25    wait_for_animation
26    click("go", :id)
27    wait_for_ajax
```

Before we start to refactor all of the code duplication into the Action Wrapper pattern, let's make sure our test is now passing. The test output should look like this:

```
# Running tests:

.

Finished tests in 10.943344s, 0.0914 tests/s, 0.0914 assertions/s.

1 tests, 1 assertions, 0 failures, 0 errors, 0 skips
```

The Action Wrapper pattern

The idea behind the Action Wrapper pattern is to collect all of the most common pain points, such as AJAX, and automatically implement them every time that action is performed. It helps to future proof the tests by automatically accounting for things that commonly go wrong and destabilizing the tests.

Advantages of the Action Wrapper pattern

The Action Wrapper pattern has a lot more advantages than disadvantages; let's take a look at them:

- **Single location for actions**: All of the actions such as clicking, typing, and dealing with AJAX requests and animations are in a single class. This makes them easy to find and modify and very DRY.

 The DRY principle and the DRY pattern are discussed in *Chapter 3, Refactoring Tests.*

- **Increased overall build stability**: Overall, the test suite becomes a lot more stable since forgetting to add a wait no longer breaks random tests at random times.

- **Capture and append exceptions**: If an action (such as clicking on a button) cannot be performed, we can capture the stack trace and add more information for better debugging.

- **Helps to implement screenshot pattern**: This pattern makes it easier to add functionality that will capture screenshots of the whole web page on test failures.

Disadvantages of the Action Wrapper pattern

The biggest disadvantage of the Action Wrapper pattern is increased time. We are trading fast build time for a more stable build, which is typically a good trade.

> The build time increase is not that dramatic. If intelligent delays are implemented properly, we will be adding 10 percent to 20 percent time increase, while reducing test flakiness by up to 80 percent.

Implementing the Action Wrapper pattern

By using the Wrapper pattern on the Selenium class, we are able to add some additional functionality to our test actions. A click on the **Purchase** button does not have to be just a click; it can become so much more. Wrapping an action gives us the ability to ask the AJAX and animations to finish after we click on any button automatically. Furthermore, we are able to catch any exception in our test and take a screenshot of the whole page at that moment in order to help us debug the failure!

> The Wrapper pattern, also called **Decorator pattern** or **Adapter pattern**, is a design pattern used to encapsulate certain objects to give them more functionality than initially designed. For example, in Selenium, the `click` method and the `save_screenshot` methods are separate entities. By wrapping the `click` method, we are able to attempt a click and take an instant screenshot of the webpage if the click fails for any reason whatsoever.

To save some time, I did some refactoring for us, so please download the new project from here `http://awful-valentine.com/code/chapter-5`. To make the project files more manageable, I created several new folders and grouped files inside. Let's look at the new places for everything, starting with all the files that deal with test data. They now live in the `fixtures` directory as shown here:

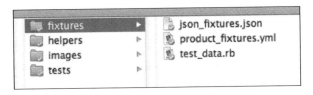

All of the tests we have written so far now live in the `tests` directory, as shown here:

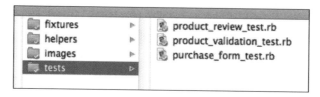

The `images` directory is where we will store screenshots of the web page on test failures, but right now it is empty. Finally, the `helpers` directory, shown in the following screenshot, is where we will store the `selenium_wrapper.rb`. We will implement the Action Wrapper pattern in this file:

The `SeleniumWrapper` class will become a single point of contact between the tests and the web page being tested. Let's take a look at this class in detail; we will start with methods responsible for the creation and destruction of browser sessions:

```ruby
require 'selenium-webdriver'

class SeleniumWrapper
  def initialize(browser = :firefox)
    @selenium = Selenium::WebDriver.for(browser)
  end

  def quit
    @selenium.quit
  end
```

The initializer method creates a new instance of `WebDriver` with a chosen `browser` that defaults to Firefox. It stores this new session in the `@selenium` instance variable for future uses, such as when the `quit` command is invoked.

Since waiting for AJAX and animations to complete is a common task in every test, we moved those methods into `SeleniumWrapper` class, as shown here:

```
11
12    def wait_for_ajax
13      Selenium::WebDriver::Wait.new(:timeout => 60).until do
14        sleep 1
15        @selenium.execute_script("return jQuery.active") == 0
16      end
17    end
18
19    def wait_for_animation
20      Selenium::WebDriver::Wait.new(:timeout => 60).until do
21        sleep 1
22        @selenium.execute_script("return jQuery(':animated').length") == 0
23      end
24    end
25
```

Since will be using these methods a lot, let's make a small method called `wait_for_ajax_and_animation` that calls both AJAX and animation wait, as shown here:

```
25
26    def wait_for_ajax_and_animation
27        wait_for_ajax
28        wait_for_animation
29    end
30
```

Next, we moved all of the little helper methods such as `type_text` or `click` into the `SeleniumWrapper` class. This allows us to have these methods implemented only once and shared by all of the tests. However, we have modified these methods to become a lot more powerful. Let's take a look at the `type_text` method that is shown here:

```
30
31    def type_text(text, element, strategy=:css)
32      begin
33        bring_current_window_to_front
34        clear(element, strategy)
35        find_element(element, strategy).send_keys(text)
36        wait_for_ajax_and_animation
37      rescue Exception => e
38        puts "Attempt to type '#{text}' into '#{element}' with strategy '#{strategy}' has failed"
39        screenshot
40        raise e
41      end
42    end
43
```

This may seem confusing at first, but the send_keys method we used so many times before is still present on line **35**. Let's discuss the new code that surrounds the send_keys method.

On line **33**, we added a brand new method called bring_current_window_to_front, whose only job is to locate the current browser window and bring it to the very front of the display. In certain situations, JavaScript is not properly triggered when the browser in which the tests are running is not in focus. This causes some very confusing and unrepeatable test flakiness, just as AJAX requests not being triggered after we click on the **Purchase** button. By bringing the current window to the top of the screen, we sidestep this issue and improve overall test stability. For more information about bringing a browser window to the front with WebDriver, check out the blog post at http://elementalselenium.com/tips/4-work-with-multiple-windows.

Let's look at the next piece of code, line **34**. Before we start typing any text into a text field, we use the clear method to delete any text that might have been in the text box. By explicitly clearing the text boxes, we avoid situation where the new input is appended to existing text in the filed. This is especially useful on text fields that have default values in the text field that need to be overwritten.

> While writing this section of the book, I did a little experiment. I ran all of the tests on my computer 20 times to see how many would fail with the previously described JavaScript malfunctions. Out of the 20 runs, I had seven test failures due to flakiness. After adding the bring_current_window_to_front and clear methods into the Action Wrapper, I only had one test failure out of 30 runs. That's a huge stability improvement with a single line of code!

After the test finished typing text into the text field, we call the wait_for_ajax_and_animation method, as shown on line **36**. This is to allow any animation or AJAX requests to finish. This is extremely useful when testing input fields that use AJAX to auto complete text as the user types it.

The most important part of this action wrapper is the exception handling built in around each action. Typically, if the WebDriver click or send_keys encounter any difficulty, such as an element not being visible, an exception would be raised and the test exists. By wrapping these methods in begin/rescue statements, as shown in the following screenshot, we are able to print out more information about the failure and take a screenshot of the web page:

```
30
31   def type_text(text, element, strategy=:css)
32     begin
33       bring_current_window_to_front
34       clear(element, strategy)
35       find_element(element, strategy).send_keys(text)
36       wait_for_ajax_and_animation
37     rescue Exception => e
38       puts "Attempt to type '#{text}' into '#{element}' with strategy '#{strategy}' has failed"
39       screenshot
40       raise e
41     end
42   end
43
```

The test will still fail when it encounters a problem but will print out information about what it was trying to do. Furthermore, a screenshot is incredibly helpful when debugging a test in CI. We will not go into the details of every method implemented in the SeleniumWrapper class since all of the code in that class should be familiar. Let's take a look at the refactored purchase form test we have been working on this chapter. As you can see in the following screenshot, the overall size of the test file has shrunk as a lot of boilerplate and duplicate code has been moved out to a central location:

```
1
2  class PurchaseFormTests < Test::Unit::TestCase
3    def setup
4      @selenium = SeleniumWrapper.new
5    end
6
7    def teardown
8      @selenium.quit
9    end
10
11   def test_fillout_purchase_form
12     @selenium.get(TestData.get_base_url + "/purchase-forms/slow-animation")
13
14     @selenium.type_text(TestData.get_full_name, "name", :id)
15     @selenium.type_text(TestData.get_credit_card_number, "cc", :id)
16     @selenium.type_text(TestData.get_credit_card_expiry_date.month, "month", :id)
17     @selenium.type_text(TestData.get_credit_card_expiry_date.year, "year", :id)
18
19     @selenium.click("go", :id)
20     assert_equal("Purchase complete!", @selenium.get_inner_text("success", :id))
21   end
22 end
```

The final change has been an addition of the `runt_tests.rb` file. We moved all of the boilerplate `require` statements that used to be in every test here. We no longer need to run each test file individually; instead, we can run the full test suite by simply running this command:

```
ruby run_tests.rb
```

The result of this command should be all of the tests executing with the help of the `SeleniumWrapper` class. The result of running all of the tests should look like this:

```
Run options:

# Running tests:

.....

Finished tests in 146.313326s, 0.0342 tests/s, 0.3759 assertions/s.

5 tests, 55 assertions, 0 failures, 0 errors, 0 skips
```

Our test suite is now in a much better place. We protected it from a lot of flakiness due to JavaScript and browser idiosyncratic issues. There is one more type of flakiness we need protect our tests from, failures due to unnecessary third-party dependencies. The Black Hole Proxy pattern is used to help with these.

The Black Hole Proxy pattern

The Black Hole Proxy pattern tries to reduce test instability by getting rid of as many third-party uncertainties as possible. Modern websites have a lot of third-party content loaded on every page. There are social networking buttons, images coming from CDNs, tracking pixels, and much more. All of these items can destabilize our tests at any point. Black Hole Proxy takes all HTTP requests going to third-party websites and blocks them, as if the request was sucked into a black hole.

> Web pages that have heavy traffic in the production environment tend to cache their JavaScript and the cached assets on a third-party CDN. When testing an environment such as production, we should not be blocking critical assets but allowing them to be properly loaded using the proxy whitelist feature.

Advantages of the Black Hole Proxy pattern

Black Hole Proxy brings many advantages to our tests:

- **Improved speed**: Since the web applications we test tend to be on the local network, the web page loads are much faster if there is no wait for third-party content to load.

- **Improved stability**: Modern web applications have a lot of third-party dependencies that are not critical to core functionality of the application. These include tracking pixels and social media buttons, such as Facebook or Twitter. Sometimes, these third-party dependencies will make our tests fail because they are taking a longer than usual amount of time to load. Blocking these noncritical third-party dependencies allow our Selenium tests to verify the functionality of our application without breaking due to unpredictable dependencies.

- **Hermetically sealed tests**: The test has higher control over the environment. By blocking third-party content, we reduce external dependencies that cause test failures.

Disadvantages of the Black Hole Proxy pattern

There are two major disadvantages to the Black Hole Proxy pattern:

- **Broken layout**: If a lot of third-party content is removed from the page, the page will still function, but the locations of buttons and images might shift to fill out the newly created gaps on the page.

- **Third-party content tests are broken**: Any test that tries to check the third-party integration, such as logging in with social network credentials, will not work. We have to implement a way to give the tests control over the Black Hole Proxy pattern.

Implementing the Black Hole Proxy pattern

Our website integrates with a couple of third-party social networks. The **A** book is a social network for people whose name start with the letter A. The **Walker** network is for sending 142 character status updates to your walking buddies. Both of the networks are integrated at random spots of our application. Furthermore, our website has two banners on every page. Overall, our purchase form page looks something like this:

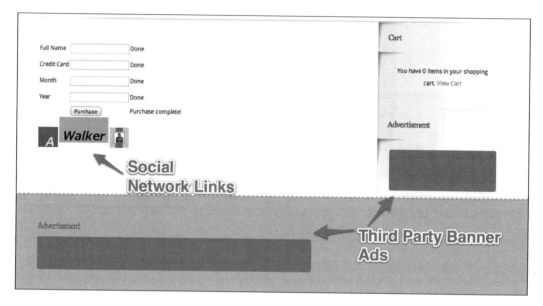

Our social network partners are having a slow network connection. To simulate that, let's modify the `PurchaseFormTests` test once more. We change the first line of the test to navigate to a new page that has a lot of slow loading third-party dependencies, as shown in the preceding image. Let's modify our test's target URL like this:

```
11  def test_fillout_purchase_form
12    @selenium.get(TestData.get_base_url + "/purchase-forms/3rd-party-links")
13
```

This new URL takes us to a page that is designed to simulate extremely slow loading third-party assets such as social network sites and tracking pixels. If we run our test suite now, we will get `Timeout::Error`, as shown in the following screenshot, because the tests timed out while waiting for the page to finish loading. An uncontrollable delay is caused by third-party dependencies:

```
Timeout::Error: Timeout::Error
    /Users/dima/.rvm/gems/ruby-1.9.3-p362@book/gems/selenium-webdriver-2.42.0/lib/selenium/webdriver/remote/http/default.rb:83:in `response_for'
    /Users/dima/.rvm/gems/ruby-1.9.3-p362@book/gems/selenium-webdriver-2.42.0/lib/selenium/webdriver/remote/http/default.rb:39:in `request'
    /Users/dima/.rvm/gems/ruby-1.9.3-p362@book/gems/selenium-webdriver-2.42.0/lib/selenium/webdriver/remote/http/common.rb:40:in `call'
    /Users/dima/.rvm/gems/ruby-1.9.3-p362@book/gems/selenium-webdriver-2.42.0/lib/selenium/webdriver/remote/bridge.rb:634:in `raw_execute'
```

We will be taking advantage of the HTTP proxy settings that all browsers use. Our tests will send all of the HTTP traffic, without our testing environment, to a fake proxy that will swallow up all of the requests. Let's add a couple of lines to the class initializer:

```ruby
 4    def initialize(browser = :firefox)
 5      profile = Selenium::WebDriver::Firefox::Profile.new
 6      profile["network.proxy.type"]          = 1
 7      profile["network.proxy.http"]          = "127.0.0.1"
 8      profile["network.proxy.http_port"]     = 9999
 9      profile["network.proxy.no_proxies_on"] = "localhost, 127.0.0.1, *awful-valentine.com"
10      @selenium = Selenium::WebDriver.for(browser, :profile => profile)
11    end
```

The preceding code performs the following actions:

- It creates an instance of the `Firefox::Profile` class
- It configures the HTTP proxy to point to a non existing proxy on 127.0.0.1 with port of 9999

> You do not have to use a fake proxy at all. As a matter of fact, you can create a simple proxy server that logs all external URLs to a logfile. This way you know all the external dependencies in your application. Just make sure that no matter what the request is, your proxy server returns a 200 response with an empty body. BrowserMob Proxy accomplishes just that, and it can be found at `http://bmp.lightbody.net/`.

- It tells the profile to not use the proxy for any connections going to `localhost`, `127.0.0.1`, and all instances of our website
- Finally, it tells Selenium to get us a new instance of Firefox with the profile we just made

Let's run the test suite again. All the tests should be passing, like this:

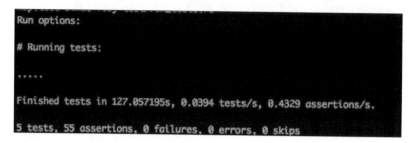

When loading the web page, here is what the tests see:

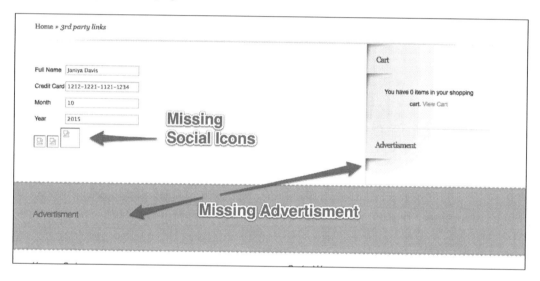

The tests are now at the highest stability point they have ever been. Some flakiness will occur from time to time; this cannot be avoided. However, the more work we put in stabilizing our Selenium tests, the fewer failures we will see. At some point in the future, when the Selenium build fails, we will have confidence to say it is a real bug that caused the failure and not test flakiness.

Test your tests!

A last thought before we close this chapter: not enough time and thought is given to the idea of testing the tests themselves. One should not hurry in adding a new test to the suite without running it at least a dozen times. Personally, I tend to run each new test about 20 times before I consider it stable. Just put the tests in a loop, let it run for 20 minutes while you get a cup of coffee. You will be surprised how often a test will fail if you just let it run enough times.

Finally, don't forget to test your tests on multiple browsers. As a rule of the thumb, any test you will write will be a lot more stable in Firefox and Chrome browsers than they are in Internet Explorer and Safari. Just because you got stability in the test suite for the first two browsers, it does not mean the latter two are stable.

Summary

In this chapter, we covered the topic of test stability. We discussed some of the things that make an individual test stable—starting with cultural changes on the team and ending with changing personal behavior, such as testing our own tests before committing them to source control.

We also discussed some of the more technical solutions such as using an existing JavaScript infrastructure to check completion of background AJAX requests and JavaScript animations. We also wrapped some of the common Selenium actions to automatically give them the ability to wait for JavaScript events and take a full-page screenshot of the page when something fails.

Now that we have some measure of stability in our tests, we can start spending more time thinking about the test declaration versus test implementation. In the next chapter, we will be testing the behavior of our application.

6
Testing the Behavior

"Do not allow watching food to replace making food."

-Alton Brown

How important is it to clearly state your intended actions? When driving a car on an empty street at night, do you use a turning signal to let any unseen pedestrians know what you intend to do? It is too easy to write a test that seems fine, but after two months of working on something else, it looks completely cryptic and incomprehensible.

In this chapter, we will be converting our tests from a cryptic set of method calls into something that any person off the street can understand. The actions of the test will remain the same, but how each action is described will become dramatically clearer. In this chapter, we will cover the following topics:

- Behavior-driven Development
- The write once, test everywhere pattern
- JBehave
- Cucumber

Behavior-driven Development

Writing a test that clearly states its intent, is useful in itself. However, as we get into the habit of making ourselves clearly understood, we start to notice a pattern. **Behavior-driven Development (BDD)** encourages us to step back and think of how the application should behave end-to-end first, and only then concentrate on the smaller details. After all, our application can be refactored many times with all of the IDs and names changing while still maintaining the same intended behavior.

Advantages of BDD

By separating the implementation details from the behavior definition, our tests gain a lot of advantages:

- **Better test understanding**: If the test is written properly, then it is possible to know exactly what the test plans to do without being confused by code details.

- **Modular implementation**: The methods that perform the actual implementation can be shared while testing.

 For more information on code reuse, see the *The DRY testing pattern* section in *Chapter 3, Refactoring Tests*.

- **Versatile implementation options**: By sticking closely to behavior, it is easy to have one defined behavior running in multiple environments. This will further be explained in the write once, test everywhere pattern later in this chapter.

- **Multiple BDD frameworks**: There are multiple testing frameworks written to allow you to test with the BDD principle in just about every programming language.

- **Data separation**: Data used by the test is extracted out of the behavior definition, making it easier to manage the data in the long run.

 To study further, refer to the *Hardcoding input data* section in *Chapter 4, Data-driven Testing*.

Disadvantages of BDD

There are several disadvantages of using BDD tools; some teams might find that the negatives outweigh the positives. Here are some examples of the disadvantages of BDD:

- **Consistent specification language**: If you ask 10 people to describe a spoon in one sentence, you will get 10 different sentences. Having the whole team agree on how a registration flow should be described in a consistent plain language can be a nightmare. Without having a consistent standard, it is easy to create duplicate code based on how someone wishes to describe an action. For example, `I click on the product link` and `I follow the link to product page` could be describing the same method call.

Gojko Adzic describes ways to bridge the communication gap between team members in *Specification by Example: How Successful Teams Deliver the Right Software*, Manning Publications.

- **Easy to mix behavior and implementation**: It is very temptingly easy to start adding implementation into a definition. This practice leads to muddled, confused, and hardcoded tests.

- **Which BDD tool to use**: Any team might have a long and heated debate over which tool is perfect for a project. Choosing the perfect tool might be very difficult.

- **Added overhead**: Adding another framework to a project makes writing tests simpler. However, each tool will use precious resources such as time or processing power.

- **Learning curve**: Each new framework will have a learning curve before everyone on the team can use the tools effectively.

Testing the shopping cart behavior

Adding items to the shopping cart is one of the key components of any online store test suite. This test has to be one of the most common tests ever written. It is a crucial part of our website and lies directly on the *Money Path* of the application.

 Money Path is a simple concept; it says that it is okay to have an occasional bug go into production, as long as none of these bugs ever prevent the customer from giving us their money. A customer might forgive a bug that prevents them from uploading a profile picture, but won't be so forgiving if they cannot purchase the item they desperately need. For more information on this, please refer to the *The money path suite* section in *Chapter 8, Growing the Test Suite*.

If we were to write a test that adds a product to a cart, it might look something like this:

```
1  def test_add_item_to_cart
2    @selenium.get(TestData.get_base_url + "/our-love-is-special")
3    @selenium.click("single-addtocart", :class)
4    @selenium.click("addToCart_3", :id)
5
6    assert_equal("$68.99", @selenium.get_inner_text("grand-total-amount", :class))
7    assert_equal("You have 1 item ($68.99) in your shopping cart.",
8              @selenium.get_inner_text("Cart66WidgetCartEmptyAdvanced", :id))
9  end
10
```

Let's walk through the actions of this test, starting with line **2**:

1. Navigate to the page of the product we wish to test by using the `get` method and our `TestData` class to obtain the environment URL.

2. Click on the initial **Add To Cart** button, as follows, that has a CSS class of `.single-addtocart`:

3. After a modal giving more description appears on the screen, the test clicks on another **Add to Cart** button. The JavaScript modal looks like this:

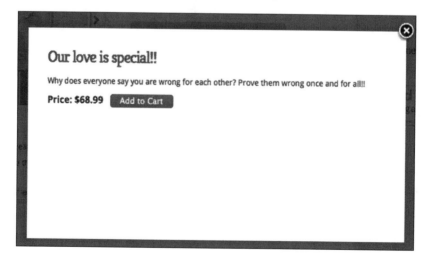

After the modal is displayed, the test clicks on the second **Add to Cart** button.

 Note that the JavaScript modal shown here is drawn with jQuery. Because our tests are using the Action Wrapper pattern discussed in *Chapter 5, Stabilizing the Tests*, they automatically wait for everything to be on the screen before clicking on the second **Add to Cart** button.

4. Finally, the test asserts the total amount due, which resides in a DIV with the class `grand-total-amount`. Then, it checks the human-readable summary of the cart from the DIV with the ID `Cart66WidgetCartEmptyAdvanced`. The cart summary page is shown as follows:

This test is quite brief, concise, and to the point. It is easy to call it complete and move on to another test all together. However, let's take a look at some of the problems with this test:

- The test's class name and test name are the only things telling us what the overall goal of the test is. Even though they are short and concise, they don't really explain what the test is doing.

- Individual steps are written in pure code, without a step-by-step explanation of what each line does; a non-technical individual will have a hard time understanding what is going on.

- Every class and ID of the HTML elements in the test is hard coded, and by now we all know that hardcoding is difficult to maintain and causes long-term difficulties.

Describing shopping cart behavior

To solve similar issues with tests, Dan North set out to develop a new way to describe application behavior in the *Given, When, Then* format.

For more information about Dan North and BDD, you can visit his website `http://dannorth.net`. His article *Introducing BDD* is a must read, and can be found at `http://dannorth.net/introducing-bdd`.

This textual format template gives semirigid rules to be used when describing any feature. For example, the `add to cart` test can be described as a human-like language called Gherkin. Let's take a look at this test translated into Gherkin:

```
Feature: users can add products to their shopping cart.

Scenario: Anonymous user adds product to the cart
  Given an anonymous user is on a product page
  When they add the item to their cart

  Then will see "$68.99" in the grand total section
  And they will see a cart summary with "You have 1 item ($68.99) in your shopping cart."
```

Dan's format quickly became one of the most popular formats to describe feature behaviors. There are dozens of tools written in every major computer language, which parse this format and implement actual test steps based on it. Let's take a closer look at the keywords used in this format:

- **Features**: This give an overview of the whole feature. It is used to describe a group of `Scenarios` in a given test file.

- **Scenario**: This describes different test variations within the overall features. Here are a couple of `Scenarios` for our feature:

  ```
  Scenario: Anonymous user adds product to the cart
  Scenario: Logged in user adds product to the cart
  Scenario: User adds a non-existing product to the cart
  ```

- **Given**: This is the starting point of the test; it describes preconditions that need to be in place before the test can successfully start.

To say that a `Given` statement is analogous to a `setup` method is not entirely correct. Yes, it is used to put our environment into a certain state before the actual test begins, but individual scenarios can have different `Given` statements. Some BDD frameworks support the concept of the `Background` statement, which resembles a `setup` method.

- **When**: These statements are used to start performing actions against the current state of the application. In this case, we click on the **Add To Cart** button.

- **Then**: These statements are used to describe the final state of the application; they are used as a test assertion.

- **And**: These statements are usually interchangeable between `Given`, `When`, or `Then`. They are there to allow the feature description flow naturally in a human language. The preceding feature description can be typically rewritten as shown in the following screenshot:

```
Scenario: Anonymous user adds product to the cart
  Given an anonymous user is on a product page
  When they add the item to their cart

  Then will see "$68.99" in the grand total section
  Then they will see a cart summary with "You have 1 item ($68.99) in your shopping cart."
```

Writing step definitions

We now have a declaration of how our application is supposed to behave in a human language. We are ready to concentrate on implementing a test for this feature.

 Typically, a step is any line item that performs some action in our application. Scenarios and features are not steps in traditional ways, as they only clarify the behavior and do not perform any work.

Let's take a look at how each step is implemented one at a time:

- We start with the `Given` step, which sets up the environment in a testable state. In this case, it navigates to a certain URL:

```
Given(/^an anonymous user is on a product page$/) do
  @selenium.get(TestData.get_base_url + "/our-love-is-special")
end
```

- Next, we implement the two separate steps that click on the **Add to Cart** buttons:

```
When(/^they add the item to their cart$/) do
  @selenium.click("single-addtocart", :class)
  @selenium.click("addToCart_3", :id)
end
```

- Our test concludes with a `Then` step, which checks that the application behaved in a predictable manner:

```
Then(/^will see "(.*?)" in the grand total section$/) do |price|
  assert_equal(price, @selenium.get_inner_text("grand-total-amount", :class))
end

Then(/^they will see a cart summary with "(.*?)"$/) do |cart_summary|
  assert_equal(cart_summary, @selenium.get_inner_text("Cart66WidgetCartEmptyAdvanced", :id))
end
```

If we compare the code that does the actual testing, we can see that our step definitions are identical to the test we wrote earlier in the chapter. This is the biggest power and strength of most BDD frameworks; they allow users to write real programming language code, not just a specially formatted XML. The step names do use the *Given, When, Then* format but inside each step is pure Ruby. However, what if we need to use another language besides Ruby to write our tests? Luckily for us, the majority of the programming languages have an implementation of this BDD definition format. Let's take a look at a couple of examples for the `Then I should see "$68.99" in the grand total section` step written in several languages besides Ruby:

Language	Code Example

Java with JBehave framework	`@Then("I should see $price in the grand total section")`
	`public void theGridShouldLookLike(String price) {`
	    `//Assertion of price`
	`}`

Python with Lettuce framework	`@step('I should see "(\$[\d\.]+)" in the grand total section')`
	`def see_the_string_in_grand_total_section(step, price):`
	    `#Assertion`

PHP with Behat framework	`/**`
	 `* @Then /^I should see "(\$[\d\.]+)" in the grand total section$/`
	 `*/`
	`public function iSeePriceInGrandTotal($price)`
	`{`
	  `/* Assertion */`
	`}`

Is BDD right for my project?

Each project and team is different, so choosing the right test framework should be an informed decision. As you are trying to make this decision, ask yourself a couple of questions:

- **Is BDD too much for what you need?:** Sometimes, the project you are working on is too small or simple to set up a large BDD framework. If you do not expect any growth in the project and test suite, maybe a simple test written in plain language is more than enough.

  "Do not use a cannon to kill a mosquito."

  -Confucius

- **Is human language too nuanced?:** Using plain-language step definitions has a lot of downfalls. For example, the `I should be able to Click Purchase button`, `I Click Purchase button`, and `Purchase button should be clickable` step definitions can be phrased in many other ways. Can the whole team agree on how to describe every action in the future so that duplication is not caused?

- **Do you have a proper IDE to deal with Regular Expressions?:** To make the step definitions reusable, you might need to use a lot of regular expressions to get different variables out of a name. Searching the project to see whether a step has already been defined is extremely complicated if you do not have an IDE to autocomplete the already defined steps.

- **Is the Given, When, Then format right for you?:** Being able to read the test intention in human language is great. However, if you do not plan to ever have any nontechnical individual people read the tests, maybe implementing another framework is too much when a simple Test::Unit or JUnit will suffice.

Introducing Cucumber

Cucumber is a tool used to convert BDD behavior definitions into executable steps in several programming languages besides Ruby. Similar to the tools mentioned in the previous section, it parses the *Given, When, Then* format of feature specification and matches it with the proper code implementation. Cucumber has many great features that we will now explore. To save time, the majority of the existing test suites have been converted to Cucumber already; please download the new workspace from `http://awful-valentine.com/code/chapter-6/part-1`.

Our workspace project structure has changed a little bit to accommodate some of the cucumber conventions. Let's take a look how the files are now arranged:

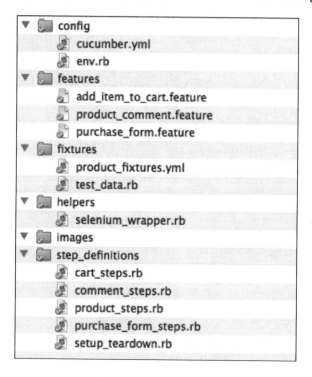

As you can see, the test suite structure has not changed much from what it used to be in the previous chapter, except a couple of files were moved and renamed, and several were deleted. Let's take a closer look at the Cucumber-specific changes.

Feature files

The `features` directory has several files with the `.feature` extension. These are the files with the *Given, When, Then* style of feature definitions. Take a look inside them and make sure all of our tests make sense in a human-readable language.

> One of the great features of Cucumber is that it's not tied to the English language. If you wanted to write your feature definition in Russian or Japanese, there is nothing stopping you from accomplishing that. For more information on the supported spoken languages, visit Cucumber's wiki page at `https://github.com/cucumber/cucumber/wiki/Spoken-languages`.

Step definition files

The `step_definitions` directory contains all the Ruby files that implement the steps described in the `.feature` files. Steps defined in any of these files automatically become globally accessible to the whole test suite. It is a standard practice to name the `_steps.rb` files as clearly as possible because that will help everyone find the required step much faster. For example, any steps definitions that have to deal with creating a comment will go into `review_steps.rb`.

 Typically, the `step_definitions` directory should be placed inside the `features` directory. By following this standard, all the files in the `step_definitions` directory will be automatically required for runtime. However, for reasons that will become clear later in this chapter, we will ignore this convention for now and explicitly use the `step_definitions` directory.

The `setup_teardown.rb` file contains the two blocks of code that start a new browser before each test and quit the browser after the test has finished executing.

 A common practice with Cucumber is to put the global `Before` and `After` steps into the `env.rb` file. However, I would advise against this practice since this file can grow to be incredibly large and difficult to manage; using smaller well-named files is much better for everyone involved.

These blocks of code look like this:

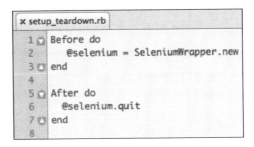

```
setup_teardown.rb

1  Before do
2      @selenium = SeleniumWrapper.new
3  end
4
5  After do
6      @selenium.quit
7  end
8
```

The configuration directory

The configuration directory is a reserved directory in Cucumber; inside, you will typically find the configuration for our test suite. The convention is to store anything that is related to how the tests are executed in this directory.

Cucumber.yml

The `cucumber.yml` file is one of the files that is used to store Cucumber profiles. Currently, our file looks like this:

```
<%
  common_requires = "--require config --require step_definitions"
%>

default: <%= common_requires %> --format pretty
ci: <%= common_requires %> --format progress
```

 `cucumber.yml` can be written in plain YAML format or in ERB, which is a template language used to insert Ruby code inside YAML and some other files. Ruby code lives within the `<%` and `%>` characters.

The `cucumber.yml` files begins by collecting all of the directories that contain the required Ruby files into the `common_requires` variable. Then, it specifies two profiles, `default` and `ci`, which in turn incorporate the `common_requires` variable.

In this example, the only difference between the profiles is the format in which the test results are printed out. When a profile is not specified, the `default` profile's `pretty` formatter will look like this:

```
Using the default profile...
Feature: The shopping cart should be able to accept products chosen by user.

  Scenario: Anonymous user adds product to the cart                                    # features/add_item_to_cart.feature:3
    Given I am on a product page                                                       # step_definitions/product_steps.rb:1
    When I click on Add To Cart button                                                 # step_definitions/cart_steps.rb:1
    And I click on the Add to Cart button in the product description modal              # step_definitions/cart_steps.rb:5
    Then I should see "$58.99" in the grand total section                              # step_definitions/cart_steps.rb:9
      <"$58.99"> expected but was
      <"$68.99">. (MiniTest::Assertion)
      ./step_definitions/cart_steps.rb:10:in `/^I should see "(\$[\d\.]+)" in the grand total section$/'
      features/add_item_to_cart.feature:8:in `Then I should see "$58.99" in the grand total section'
    And I should see "You have 1 item ($68.99) in your shopping cart." in the cart summary # step_definitions/cart_steps.rb:13

Feature: A product page should be able to accept user generated comments.

  Background:                        # features/product_comment.feature:3
    Given I am on a product page     # step_definitions/product_steps.rb:1

  Scenario: Adding new comment                            # features/product_comment.feature:7
    When I create a new unique comment                    # step_definitions/comment_steps.rb:1
    Then my name should be attached to the comment         # step_definitions/comment_steps.rb:7
    And my comment should be properly saved                # step_definitions/comment_steps.rb:11
    And the comment date should be correct date            # step_definitions/comment_steps.rb:15

  Scenario: Adding a duplicate comment should be rejected # features/product_comment.feature:14
    When I create a new unique comment                    # step_definitions/comment_steps.rb:1
    And I try to add an identical comment again            # step_definitions/comment_steps.rb:23
    Then I should see a duplicate comment error            # step_definitions/comment_steps.rb:27

Feature: As a user, I should be able to fill out the purchase form and successfully complete a purchase

  Scenario: User fills out purchase form with valid results # features/purchase_form.feature:3
    Given I am on the purchase page                         # step_definitions/purchase_form_steps.rb:1
    And I submit valid values on the purchase form           # step_definitions/purchase_form_steps.rb:5
    Then I should have a successful purchase transaction     # step_definitions/purchase_form_steps.rb:14

Failing Scenarios:
cucumber features/add_item_to_cart.feature:3 # Scenario: Anonymous user adds product to the cart

4 scenarios (1 failed, 3 passed)
17 steps (1 failed, 1 skipped, 15 passed)
1m42.454s
```

The test failure was introduced to demonstrate how the stack trace is printed out in
the `pretty` format.

The `ci` profile uses the `progress` output formatter. This type of output looks much cleaner when running our tests in CI. The test output in the `progress` formatter should look familiar, as it resembles the `Test::Unit` output first introduced in *Chapter 1, Writing the First Test*:

```
Using the ci profile...
...F-.............

(::) failed steps (::)

<"$58.99"> expected but was
<"$68.99">. (MiniTest::Assertion)
./step_definitions/cart_steps.rb:10:in `/^I should see "(\$[\d\.]+)" in the grand total section$/'
features/add_item_to_cart.feature:8:in `Then I should see "$58.99" in the grand total section'

Failing Scenarios:
cucumber -p ci features/add_item_to_cart.feature:3 # Scenario: Anonymous user adds product to the cart

4 scenarios (1 failed, 3 passed)
17 steps (1 failed, 1 skipped, 15 passed)
```

env.rb

The `env.rb` file is a bit of a catchall file. We typically store global variables, gem requirements, and anything else the whole test suite would need access to. This saves us the trouble of requiring a specific gem in every single step definition file.

Running the Cucumber suite

Now that we are familiar with the project layout, let's execute some tests. To start, let's install the Cucumber gem. So, run the following command in the terminal:

```
gem install cucumber
```

After the gem has been installed, we have several commands we can use to run our tests from the root of the working directory:

1. To execute the whole suite in the `default` profile, we simply run the following command in our terminal from the root of our workspace:

    ```
    cucumber
    ```

    The Cucumber gem will automatically find the `features` directory. If your features are located in another directory, you will need to specify the path to that directory like this:

    ```
    cucumber some/other/directory
    ```

2. Use the `-p` flag to specify a different profile at the time of execution. To run our whole test suite in the `ci` profile, we can use this command:

```
cucumber -p ci
```

3. We do not need to execute the whole test suite every single time. If we want to run only a single file or all the feature files in a directory, we just provide the path to the file/directory as the last parameter in our command:

```
Cucumber -p features/add_item_to_cart.feature
```

4. Finally, we can execute just a single scenario in any feature file by appending a colon and line number of the scenario. The following commands will only execute the scenarios that are on the provided line:

```
cucumber features/product_review.feature:15

cucumber features/product_review.feature:15:33

cucumber features/product_review.feature:15 features/ add_item_to_
cart.feature:20
```

Now that you know the basics of using Cucumber, you have a chance to play around with individual tests and see how they run, or you can write a couple of scenarios yourself for practice. When you think you have a good handle on how Cucumber works, we will move to a more advanced usage of it in the next section.

The write once, test everywhere pattern

Jeff Roggers and Kristan Vingrys initially developed the write once, test everywhere pattern while working at ThoughtWorks. The concept centers on taking advantage of shared behavior between multiple implementations of one application. For example, it should be possible to purchase a product from our website no matter whether the user is using our full website, the mobile version, or native mobile application. If the feature definitions are well written, the steps used to implement the test can be interchangeable.

The write once, test everywhere pattern is also known as the pluggable test pattern, since we can plug the implementation of tests into different contexts. As we change the context from the desktop website to mobile to API tests, we plug in the correct implementation.

Advantages of the write once, test everywhere pattern

The write once, test everywhere pattern has several advantages going for it; here is a list of a few of them:

- **Foresight**: This pattern forces the architect of the test suite to think ahead and boil down every feature and behavior into the simplest, most common list of ideas. When the idea is boiled down to the most basic components, it can describe the behavior of our application from multiple implementations.

- **Reusability**: The behavior definition can be reused between the mobile website test suite, the full browser test suite, and even at times for native mobile applications. Furthermore, some of the steps written for the full browser version and mobile versions can be reused, as some of the web elements share similar attributes.

- **Simplicity**: We have a single test suite that runs on multiple platforms, and it shares some of the implementation details. There is no need to have multiple test suites.

Disadvantages of the write once, test everywhere pattern

There are, however, some disadvantages in placing multiple test suites in a single one. Let's take a look at these disadvantages:

- **Runtime context switching**: In the example provided, we use Ruby's ability to require the correct step definitions on the fly based on the profile. In static languages such as Java, this might be more difficult to accomplish.

- **Complex code base**: Combining multiple test suites into one has a lot of advantages; however, the project structure might become convoluted and difficult to understand very quickly.

Testing a mobile site

Like many other websites, ours has a special stripped down version to be used with smart phones. The ability to leave comments on any product remains, but the steps to fill up the product comment are now different. So in this section, we will make `product_review.feature` work on both regular and mobile websites. Let's update our test suite to run on both the full browser version and mobile browser version.

Typically, testing mobile versions of a website can be better accomplished by driving the tests on the actual smart phone or in an emulator. There are two good projects that allow WebDriver tests to run on mobile devices. These projects are iOS Driver and Appium. The project websites are listed respectively: `http://ios-driver.github.io/ios-driver` and `http://appium.io`. However, modifying the browser's user agent does not require as much setup time.

Updating the Selenium wrapper

Our first step is to modify how Firefox identifies itself to websites by modifying the user agent's name. Since our website decides which version to serve to the browser based on the user agent, we will change the Firefox profile to identify itself as iPhone. Let's open `selenium_wrapper.rb` and modify the `initialize` method to look like this:

```
2
3  class SeleniumWrapper
4    def initialize(browser = :firefox, mobile = false)
5      profile = Selenium::WebDriver::Firefox::Profile.new
6      profile["network.proxy.type"]           = 1
7      profile["network.proxy.http"]           = "127.0.0.1"
8      profile["network.proxy.http_port"]      = 9999
9      profile["network.proxy.no_proxies_on"] = "localhost, 127.0.0.1, *awful-valentine.com"
10     profile["general.useragent.override"]  = "iPhone" if mobile
11     @selenium = Selenium::WebDriver.for(browser, :profile => profile)
12   end
13
```

The `initialize` method now accepts an optional `mobile` parameter that is set to `false`, by default. If the mobile parameter is set to `true`, then we set the `general.useragent.override` parameter in the `profile` to `iPhone`.

Moving step definition files

Many of the steps that were defined for the full browser version of the application will work just fine with the mobile version, but there are several steps that will fail. So, we will make our mobile tests and full browser tests share as many steps as possible. Let's update our step definitions as follows:

1. Create a new folder called `common_steps` inside the `step_definitions` folder.

2. Move all of the `_steps.rb` files from the root of the `step_definitions` folder into the `common_steps` folder.

3. Add two new folders inside the `step_definitions` folder called `desktop` and `mobile`.

4. Add a file for each of the new directories called `setup_teardown.rb`.

5. In the `desktop` version of `setup_teardown.rb`, add the following code:

```
Before do
    @selenium = SeleniumWrapper.new
end
```

6. In the `mobile` version of `setup_teardown.rb`, add the following code:

```
Before do
    @selenium = SeleniumWrapper.new(:firefox, true)
end
```

 The mobile version of `Before` will now pass in the `mobile = true` parameter explicitly, while the desktop version will remain as it is.

7. Finally, delete the `Before` statement from `setup_teardown.rb` in the `common_steps` folder, since each version of the browser will create its own instance of `@selenium`. The file should now look like this:

```
After do
  @selenium.quit
end
```

The final layout of the `step_definitions` folder should look like this:

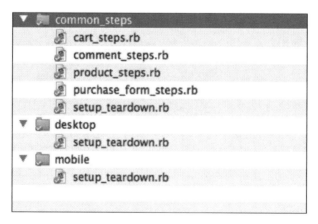

Updating the Cucumber profile and tagging tests

The final step in our refactoring effort is to identify several tests that are mobile-browser ready, and create a profile that will only execute mobile-ready tests.

To tag `product_review.feature` and `purchase_form.feature` as mobile ready, add the `@mobile` tag to the very top of each test. Both files should look something like this at the top:

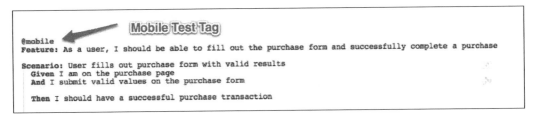

Next, we modify `cucumber.yml` to look like this:

```
x cucumber.yml

1   <%
2      config_requires = "--require config --require step_definitions/common_steps "
3
4      desktop_requires = config_requires + "--require step_definitions/desktop"
5      mobile_requires = config_requires + "--require step_definitions/mobile"
6      api_requires = "--require config --require step_definitions/api"
7   %>
8
9   default: <%= desktop_requires %> --format pretty
10  ci: <%= desktop_requires %> --format progress
11  mobile: <%= mobile_requires %> --format progress --tags @mobile
12
13
```
New mobile profile

Now we have a new `mobile` profile, which uses the `tags` parameter to only execute the tagged features of `@mobile`. Also, the `default` and `ci` profiles share `common_steps` with the `mobile` profile; at the same time, each profile requires its own appropriate folder for steps that cannot be shared.

Running and fixing incompatible steps

Our refactoring is now complete and we are ready to test both the full and mobile versions of the website. Let's first run the full browser version tests of our website by executing Cucumber with the `ci` profile:

```
cucumber -p ci
```

The result of the test run should be all the passing tests, shown as follows:

```
Using the ci profile...
.................

4 scenarios (4 passed)
17 steps (17 passed)
1m36.118s
```

Great start! Let's see whether all of the mobile tests also pass by running Cucumber in the `mobile` profile:

```
cucumber -p mobile
```

The output is as shown in the following screenshot:

```
Using the mobile profile...
...F--....

(::) failed steps (::)

Unable to locate element: {"method":"css selector","selector":"#comment-475 .comment-author-metainfo a.url"}
```

All but one of the tests passes; that's not bad at all. It turns out that the mobile version does not tag each of the comment DIVs with a unique ID. We need to rectify this difference in behavior between the full version and mobile version of our sites.

The problem comes from the `product_review.feature` file with these three steps:

```
10
11      Then my name should be attached to the comment
12      And my comment should be properly saved
13      And the comment date should be correct date
14
```

Let's fix these step definitions by separating the full browser tests from the mobile ones:

1. Create the `review_steps.rb` file in the `desktop` folder, as shown in the following screenshot:

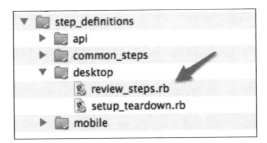

2. Move the following code out of `common_steps/review_steps.rb` into the newly created file:

```ruby
Then(/^my name should be attached to the comment$/) do
  assert_equal(@form_values[:name],
               @selenium.get_inner_text("#" + @comment_id + " .comment-author-metainfo a.url"))
end

Then(/^my comment should be properly saved$/) do
  assert_equal(@form_values[:comment], @selenium.get_inner_text("#" + @comment_id + " .comment-content"))
end

Then(/^the comment date should be correct date$/) do
  date    = @selenium.get_inner_text("#" + @comment_id + " .comment-author-metainfo .commentmetadata")
  parsed_date = DateTime.parse(date)
  assert_equal(Date.today.year, parsed_date.year)
  assert_equal(Date.today.month, parsed_date.month)
  assert_equal(Date.today.day, parsed_date.day)
end
```

3. Create the `review_steps.rb` file in the `mobile` folder:

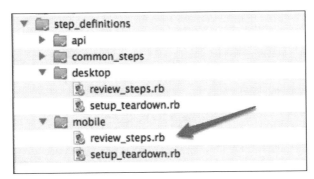

4. Add the following step implementation for the mobile browser version of `review_steps.rb`:

```ruby
Then(/^my name should be attached to the comment$/) do
    @review = @selenium.find_elements(".comment").last
    assert_equal(@form_values[:name], @review.find_element(:css, ".comment-author").text)
end

Then(/^my comment should be properly saved$/) do
    assert_equal(@form_values[:comment], @review.find_element(:css, ".comment-body").text)
end

Then(/^the comment date should be correct date$/) do
    date     = @review.find_element(:css, ".comment-time").text
    parsed_date = DateTime.parse(date)
    assert_equal(Date.today.year, parsed_date.year)
    assert_equal(Date.today.month, parsed_date.month)
    assert_equal(Date.today.day, parsed_date.day)
end

def fill_out_comment_form(form_info)
    @selenium.type_text(form_info[:name], "author", :id)
    @selenium.type_text(form_info[:email], "email", :id)
    @selenium.type_text(form_info[:website], "url", :id)
    @selenium.type_text(form_info[:comment], "comment", :id)
    @selenium.click("submit", :id)
end
```

Since the mobile view does not allow us to grab the user's review by a unique comment ID, we search for all the reviews on the page and only grab the last one created. This is seen in line **2**, in the preceding code.

> Typically, this is a very poor practice and should be avoided. If another test is running at the same time as ours, the very last review item on the page might be someone else's and not the current tests.

Now when we run the test suite in both the full browser and mobile profiles, we should see all of the tests passing:

```
mbp-3:part 2 dima$ cucumber -p ci
Using the ci profile...

................

4 scenarios (4 passed)
16 steps (16 passed)
1m43.855s
mbp-3:part 2 dima$ cucumber -p mobile
Using the mobile profile...

.............

3 scenarios (3 passed)
12 steps (12 passed)
1m27.608s
```

Testing the purchase API

Modern websites have started to include public API endpoints. These are used as a communication portal between native mobile phone applications and the core website, amongst other things. Many companies build their whole business on providing a public API. Testing the publicly accessible API is just as critical as testing the main website. After all, if the API breaks, than all of the third-party applications that consume it will stop working, thus preventing users from giving us money.

Our website provides several public API endpoints to allow third-party integration. One of these endpoints allows the purchase of a given product. By sending a POST request with some customer information, we can purchase products from a mobile phone app or a web portal embedded on some other website.

We have several options when it comes to testing our API. For example, we can write a simple shell script that will make a curl or wget request against the API endpoint and perform a simple string parsing of the resulting reply from the API. However, we already have the power of Ruby and existing Cucumber tests with the write once, test everywhere pattern. Thus, we will integrate our API tests into the existing framework.

 Curl and wget are simple command-line applications that allow users and scripts to make GET, POST, and other HTTP requests directly from the terminal or a shell script.

To get started, we will make an `HttpHelper` module that will contain the method to post data to an arbitrary URL. Our test will use the `make_post_request` method to send the customer's name, credit card info, and the ID of the product we wish to purchase. The server will return a JSON response letting us know whether the purchase was successful.

Modules (Mixins) are snippets of code and methods that do not explicitly belong to any class. Instead, any class that wishes to share these methods will include the appropriate module. This common object-oriented technique helps to reuse the code used between multiple unrelated classes.

Let's take a look at `http_helper.rb`:

```ruby
module HttpHelper

  def make_post_request(url, post_data)
    uri = URI.parse(url)
    http = Net::HTTP.new(uri.host, uri.port)
    http.open_timeout= 120
    http.read_timeout = 120
    http.continue_timeout= 120

    request = Net::HTTP::Post.new(uri.request_uri)
    request.set_form_data(post_data)

    http.request(request).body
  end

end
```

We will not go into a detailed explanation of the preceding code. The gist of the method is to take a URL string and a hash of the POST parameters, build and execute an HTTP request, and return the body of the response from the server.

To make this test more stable, we increased the request timeout to 120 seconds in case the API endpoint is under a lot of load and does not reply fast enough.

Next, we create an `api` directory inside `step_definitions`, with `purchase_steps.rb` and `setup_teardown.rb` inserted inside. So far, all of the steps performed are similar to the work we did for mobile testing support. The differences start to emerge in `setup_teardown.rb`, shown as follows:

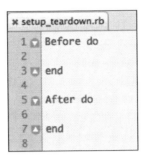

```
× setup_teardown.rb
1   Before do
2
3   end
4
5   After do
6
7   end
8
```

Since the API tests will be making direct HTTP requests against the server, we have no need for a web browser. Thus, the `Before` and `After` sections of the code are empty. Next, we need to implement the test steps in `purchase_steps.rb`. Let's take a look at the implementation of the test steps:

```
× purchase_steps.rb
1    include HttpHelper          ⟵ Telling test to use our HttpHelper
2
3    Given(/^I am on the purchase page$/) do
4        #Do nothing, because we make an HTTP request directly against and endpoint
5        #So there is no need for this step at all, but deleting it will
6        #make Cucumber think that this step is undefined
7    end
8
9    Given(/^I submit valid values on the purchase form$/) do
10       url = "http://api.awful-valentine.com/purchase"
11       @post_data = {"name" => TestData.get_full_name,
12                     "cc" => TestData.get_credit_card_number,
13                     "month" => TestData.get_credit_card_expiry_date.month,
14                     "year" => TestData.get_credit_card_expiry_date.year,
15                     "product_id" => 12345}
16
17       @purchase_status = JSON.parse(make_post_request(url, @post_data))
18   end
19
20   Then(/^I should have a successful purchase transaction$/) do
21       assert_equal(@post_data["name"], @purchase_status["name"])
22       assert_equal(@post_data["product_id"], @purchase_status["product"].to_i)
23       assert_equal("purchased", @purchase_status["status"])
24   end
25
26
```

We set the endpoint URL in line **10** and build the POST data to be sent out in line **11**. In line **17**, we send the POST request and use the `JSON.parse` method to parse the returned response from the server. We finish the test implementation by checking the returned response against expectations in lines **21** through **23**. Before we can run our API test, we just need to create a new `api` profile in `cucumber.yml`, shown as follows:

```
cucumber.yml
1  <%
2    config_requires = "--require config --require step_definitions/common_steps "
3
4    desktop_requires = config_requires + "--require step_definitions/desktop"
5    mobile_requires = config_requires + "--require step_definitions/mobile"
6    api_requires = "--require config --require step_definitions/api"
7  %>
8
9  default: <%= desktop_requires %> --format pretty
10 ci: <%= desktop_requires %> --format progress
11 mobile: <%= mobile_requires %> --format progress --tags @mobile
12 api: <%= api_requires %> --format progress --tags @api
13
14                       New api profile
```

All right, we are ready to test the API endpoint! In the following screenshot, we ran the whole test suite against the desktop, mobile, and API versions of our website. Everything should be green across the board:

```
mbp-3:part 2 dima$ cucumber -p ci && cucumber -p mobile && cucumber -p api
Using the ci profile...
.................

4 scenarios (4 passed)
16 steps (16 passed)
1m43.788s
Using the mobile profile...
............

3 scenarios (3 passed)
12 steps (12 passed)
1m27.887s
Using the api profile...
...

1 scenario (1 passed)
3 steps (3 passed)
0m0.958s
```

Summary

In this chapter, we discussed the need to test application behavior instead of implementation details. By testing the expected business behavior, our tests can still be useful in the long run, even if the underlying website is completely rewritten in a new programming language or framework. We got familiar with the BDD principle and got comfortable with a tool that implemented the BDD ideas called Cucumber. Furthermore, we used the power of our BDD tools to define our application's behavior in such a way that we are able to test both the full browser, mobile, and API versions of our application.

In the next chapter, we will discuss the page objects and how to provide a reusable framework for our tests to interact with the website.

7
The Page Objects Pattern

"There are two ways of constructing a software design: one way is to make it so simple that there are obviously no deficiencies and the other way is to make it so complicated that there are no obvious deficiencies."

-C. A. R. Hoare

Object-oriented programming (OOP) is not a new concept in computer science. It has been around since the early 1950s and has been integrated into almost every modern programming language. Selenium WebDriver is written using OOP and we have been interacting with individual objects this whole time though you might not have realized it. Even though OOP offers a lot of advantages for the code base, which we will discuss later in this chapter, a lot of tests written in Selenium do not take full advantage of it.

We are ready to take the principles and design patterns discussed throughout this book and create a fully functional Page Objects framework. To accomplish this task, we will be covering the following topics:

- Objects and OOP
- The Page Objects pattern
- The test tool independence pattern
- The YAGNI principle
- Making a test more or less intelligent

Understanding objects

If you have attended any of the Selenium conferences or read any blogs on the topic, then the topic of Page Objects must have come up multiple times. Before we get into the nitty-gritty of the Page Objects pattern implementation, let's first talk about objects.

Describing a literal object

A standard definition of an object is a material thing that can be touched, seen, and interacted with, such as a person, a car, or this book. We interact with objects on a daily basis without a second thought. Let's take a look at the cup of coffee sitting right there on your desk; tea or water if you are not a coffee drinker. Do you sit and ponder the meaning of the cup of coffee and its position within this universe? No, we just drink it, and if it's cold we reheat it or pour it into the sink as we get a new cup. By describing the temperature of the cup of coffee, we described the properties that it has. Similarly, the act of drinking out of the cup or pouring the coffee into the sink describes the actions it can perform.

Object properties

Object properties (attributes) are things that describe the current state of the object. Our cup has several attributes that we can describe with this bit of pseudocode:

```
cup = CoffeeMug
cup.color = white
cup.hight = 5 inches
cup.contents = coffee
```

 Psuedocode is an informal high-level of describing something. It concentrates on describing a complex action or algorithm in programming-like language that is human-readable.

We can go on describing all of the attributes of the drinking utensil, such as its GPS, location, or elevation above sea level. This would become too time-consuming, so instead we will talk about the things our cup can do.

Object actions

A *typical* cup, and I can't stress *typical* enough, has only one hole at the top. Through this hole, we can perform two actions with this cup; we can add liquids to the cup or we can remove them. Describing these actions with pseudocode will look like this:

```
liquid = coffee
cup.add(coffee) //Pouring fresh cup in the morning
cup.remove(1 sip) //This action would be in a loop until empty
```

Objects within objects

One last item we should discuss before moving on is that objects can store other objects as a property. The coffee inside of our mug is not part of the cup itself. Instead, it is a value of the contents attribute. We can put other objects inside the cup, such as water, juice, or tea, which all have their own attributes and their own actions. When I filled my cup of coffee up, I followed this procedure:

```
liquid = FreshCoffee
liquid.add(Sugar)
liquid.add(Milk)

cup = CoffeMug
cup.add(liquid)
```

This little analogy is not a complete waste of time, because it helps us to better understand the concept of a programming object.

Describing a programming object

In OOP, an object is an abstract representation of a data. Similar to the cup object in the preceding code, these abstract objects have properties and can perform actions known as methods. When writing automated tests, we can use the same analogy to describe just about anything we do. For example, when filling out credit card information on the purchase form, we will be using this CreditCard object:

```
card = CreditCard
card.number = 4444 3333 2222 1111
card.expiration = 01/2050
```

But why stop there? Why not use the similar analogy to describe every single page of the website we are testing?

Describing a web page with objects

Earlier in this book, in *Chapter 2, The Spaghetti Pattern*, we discussed different locator strategies to find elements on the page. By locating different elements on the page, we got a little glimpse of the hierarchy of any given page. We saw that some elements were located inside of DIVs, which were located inside of bigger DIVs, and so on. This hierarchical structuring of the web page separates different elements into groups. Let's take a look at the **Contact Us** page:

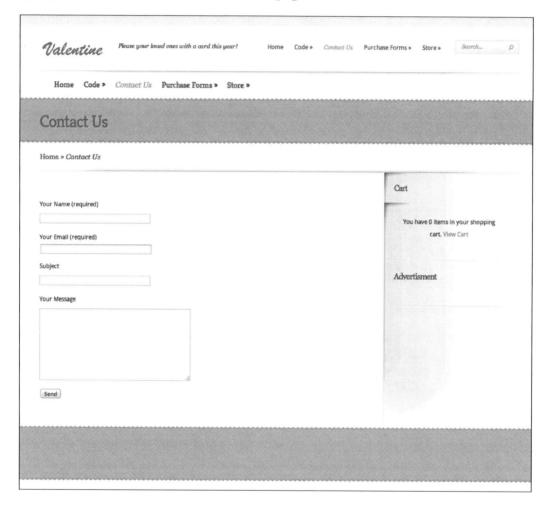

We can subdivide it into four clearly visible sections: the header, the body, the sidebar, and the footer. These sections are marked in the following image:

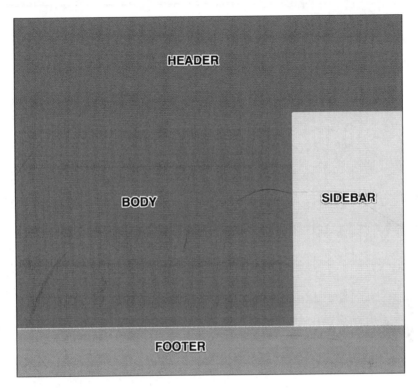

Now that the page is clearly sectioned into smaller objects, we can use a little pseudocode to describe the web page as objects:

```
page = ContactUsPage
page.header = PageHeader
page.body = PageBody
page.sidebar = PageSidebar
page.footer = PageFooter
```

Using an analogy similar to the coffee mug from earlier, we are able to describe any web page in terms of top-level objects that contain more and more granular and smaller objects within them. This style of describing a given web page is called the Page Objects pattern.

The Page Objects pattern

The Page Objects pattern describes any web page in terms of a hierarchical **Domain Specific Language (DSL)**. The application specific DSL helps to hide the page implementation; the test is no longer allowed to directly interact with a given page, but instead uses a framework of classes and methods to accomplish the same goal. This pattern abstracts the implementation details, such as element IDs, into a framework specifically designed for the application being tested.

 A DSL is a computer language that has been highly specialized for a specific application. It uses a general programming language such as Ruby or Java to implement classes and methods, which specifically apply to the application at hand.

Advantages of the Page Objects pattern

There are many advantages of using this pattern of test development; let's take a look at a handful:

- **DSL framework**: After implementing the Page Objects pattern, we end up with a framework that describes the application from business point of view. Each action performed by a test using this framework should be easy to comprehend to anyone in the given field. That is to say, a test written for an accounting system that is heavy on the field's jargon might not be easy to comprehend to the laymen; however, anyone with basic knowledge of the field should understand the intentions of each action.

 Referring to something as *business* is standard shorthand to describe the parts of the application that only the customer sees, that is, no code. The customer is anyone who uses the finished product, including people from within the company.

- **Testing behavior**: Similar to BDD, the Page Object pattern helps to test the desired behavior of the application using its DSL.

 More information about BDD can be found in *Chapter 6, Testing the Behavior*.

DRY: Unlike BDD, which has the disadvantage of phrasing a single action in multiple ways, a well-implemented and rigid Page Objects framework has one and only way to accomplish any action. This prevents duplicate implementation of the same `click` or `fill_out_form` methods.

In this context, rigidity refers to how well the rules of a framework are enforced. A flexible framework might have multiple classes or methods, which accomplish a given goal, whereas a rigid one would allow only one. Any new code that breaks this rule is not allowed.

Modular and reusable: Since each Page Object is made from multiple smaller objects, such as header section or login form, the smaller objects can be shared between multiple Page Objects.

Clear Intentions: Similar to BDD, the intended actions can be clearly represented in code. For example, a test that wishes to use the search field in the header, as shown in the following screenshot, it does not have to create a cryptic element locator search. Instead, a test that is attempting to search for `cheese` will perform an action similar to this `ContactUsPage.header.search("cheese")`. This is a lot simpler to understand than a cryptic XPATH query for the search input box.

Disadvantages of the Page Objects pattern

There are some disadvantages to this approach. Let's take a look at them:

- Complexity is increased when using Page Objects framework. As the name implies, we can't just write a simple procedural test, we need to create a framework.

- Programming design patterns should be followed to make the code consistent and easy to understand. Otherwise, the framework quickly becomes muddled and complex to use and maintain.

 A good introduction to design patterns can be found in *Design Patterns: Elements of Reusable Object-Oriented Software, Erich Gamma, Richard Helm, Ralph Johnson,* and *John Vlissides, Addison-Wesley Professional.*

- As with any new tool, it is tempting to get carried away and use it everywhere. It's tempting to implement a Page Objects framework on a test suite that only has 10 tests; this time could probably have been spent better improving existing code.

Creating a Page Objects framework

Now that we have a theoretical knowledge of Page Objects, let's put it to use. When building a new Page class, we can take multiple approaches to implement. We can use any tool that our OOP language provides for us. For this example, we will be using the inheritance as a way to quickly create new Page classes.

 Inheritance is a feature of OOP languages, which allows new classes to be based on another class, creating a subclass. The newly created subclass inherits all of the functionality of the parent class.

The majority of the web pages on our site follow a similar pattern of display: header, body, sidebar, and footer. This means we can create a generic Page class that will provide us with access to different sections of the page.

Creating a page super class

The first step of the implementation is to create a `page.rb` file that will host our class. The code inside will look like this:

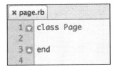

This class will provide us with access to different parts of every page. When the test needs to check the content of the shopping cart in the sidebar, it will ask the current page for the `Sidebar` object; it will ask for the `ShoppingCart` object from that object, which will provide the desired information, such as the subtotal. The code described will look something like this:

```
current_page.sidebar.cart.subtotal
```

We can implement the getter methods for the sidebar and body inside the `Page` class.

 The getter method is used to retrieve information from within an object. Since each object hides all of the properties from the rest of the world by design, it needs to have a method to retrieve the properties it wishes to share. Similarly, a setter method is used to update properties inside of the object.

I've seen multiple ways to implement the getters for different objects on the page. One approach is to break up each section into modules and have each individual page with the appropriate page section. For example, if the page containing the contact form has all four major sections, then the `ContactUsPage` class will declare this in the following manner:

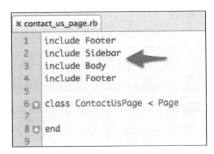

Since the error pages on our website only have a body section and no footers or headers, we would implement the `ErrorPage` class like this:

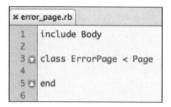

```
× error_page.rb
1    include Body
2
3    class ErrorPage < Page
4
5    end
6
```

This approach works well. However, to reduce the number of files created and referenced in this chapter, we will add the getters in the class itself:

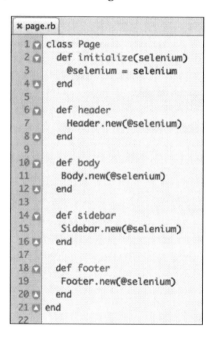

```
× page.rb
1    class Page
2      def initialize(selenium)
3        @selenium = selenium
4      end
5
6      def header
7        Header.new(@selenium)
8      end
9
10     def body
11       Body.new(@selenium)
12     end
13
14     def sidebar
15       Sidebar.new(@selenium)
16     end
17
18     def footer
19       Footer.new(@selenium)
20     end
21   end
22
```

In this chapter, we will be writing a test that adds an item into the cart and checks that the sidebar displays the said item properly. For this reason, let's implement the cod that deals with the sidebar next.

Implementing sidebar objects

Before creating a sidebar class, let's take a look at the sidebar on the page and understand the two main sections it will break into. When we have an item in the shopping cart, the sidebar looks like this:

The sidebar separates into the **Cart** and **Advertisement** sections. This means that the sidebar class will have to have two getter methods, which return the appropriate object for each section. Let's implement this in `sidebar.rb` as follows:

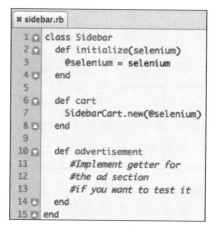

```ruby
class Sidebar
  def initialize(selenium)
    @selenium = selenium
  end

  def cart
    SidebarCart.new(@selenium)
  end

  def advertisement
    #Implement getter for
    #the ad section
    #if you want to test it
  end
end
```

Since we won't be testing the **Advertisement** section, the `advertisement` method is not implemented. We will move on to the `SidebarCart` class now.

Implementing the SidebarCart class

Let's take a closer look at the sidebar shopping cart shown in the following screenshot:

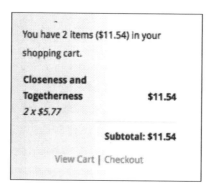

There is a lot of information displayed in such a small place. Let's divide the whole cart into smaller sections in this breakdown:

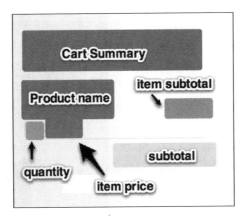

In order to access these different pieces of information, we will need to implement a getter method for each item in the `SidebarCart` class. However, we will not implement them all because of the YAGNI principle. Since our test will only check the summary and subtotal, we will only implement those methods.

 The YAGNI principle says that if you do not need something, do not implement it. If we ever write a test that examines the product name and quantity, then we will implement the getter methods at that point.

For now, the `SidebarCart` class looks like this:

```
x sidebar_cart.rb
 1  class SidebarCart
 2    def initialize(selenium)
 3      @selenium = selenium
 4    end
 5
 6    def summary
 7      @selenium.find_element(:id, "Cart66WidgetCartEmptyAdvanced").text
 8    end
 9
10    def subtotal
11        @selenium.find_element(:class, "Cart66Subtotal").text
12    end
13  end
```

Our tests are now able to interrogate the sidebar cart of any page that contains it. The test will simply follow the chain of objects until it finds the current summary or subtotal of the cart. Following this pattern, we can implement code to interact with other parts of the application. When implementing the code to interact with other parts of the application, we will keep the YAGNI principle. If we spend our time implementing a comprehensive framework instead of writing tests, we have wasted our time! The objects that were implemented in the Page Object framework but don't have a single test using them are useless. Furthermore, they quickly become obsolete when the application changes but no test failures occur to show us that the object we wrote is no longer relevant.

Adding Self Verification to pages

Not all `ElementNotVisibleError` exceptions are the same. Sometimes, the button or DIV is not present on the page because of a defect. However, there are times when the test cannot find the element because the browser is on the completely wrong page. Let's take a look at a scenario that demonstrates the second situation.

We are testing the registration flow of the application. After filling out and submitting the registration form, the page should redirect us to the account page. On the account page, our test needs to check that the username is displayed before moving on. However, our test did not notice that registration form refreshed with duplicate username error. Our test now fails with `ElementNotVisibleError`, because our test assumed that it is on account page, but in fact still is on registration page.

This type of test failure is very common and is extremely misleading. In *Chapter 5, Stabilizing the Tests*, we started to take screenshots every time any failure occurred. These screenshots will help us to understand the test failure, but what if our tests would detect that they are on the wrong page and fail with a much clearer error? Let's add a `verify` method to our `Page` class.

```
def verify(selenium)
  if URI.parse(selenium.current_url).path != page_path
    raise "Unexpected page. Expected #{page_path} but full path was #{selenium.current_url}"
  end
```

This method gets the `current_url` of the browser from Selenium and parses it with the `URI` class. Once the URL is parsed, we grab the current `path` and compare it to the value of `page_path` method; all of this is seen on line **24**. If the two paths do not match, we raise a `RuntimeError` with a helpful message that explains which page the test expected to be on, and the actual full URL in the browser. We print the full URL of the current page in case we got redirected away from our application to a new domain, such as a defect in which a link should open the target URL in a new browser window, but instead redirects in the current window.

 It might be a good idea to make the `verify` method do some other verification of the current page. The page title is another good item to verify on each page we visit.

All we have to do now is have the class initializer call the `verify` method:

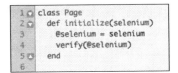

```
1  class Page
2    def initialize(selenium)
3      @selenium = selenium
4      verify(@selenium)
5    end
6
```

One last thought before moving on to implementing individual page classes: the `verify` method will check the correctness of the current page by inheriting it from the `Page` super class. If we have a one off page that does not follow the verification pattern of other pages, we can overwrite the super method and create individualized verifications for each page that needs it.

Implementing individual page classes

Now that we have a way to access different parts of individual page with the object framework and the ability to verify that we are on the correct page, it is time to start implementing individual page classes. Let's take a look at the `ContactUsPage` implementation:

```
1  class ContactUsPage < Page
2    def page_path
3      "/contact-us/"
4    end
5  end
6
```

As you can see, the amount of code required to create new page classes that adhere to the standard page layout is minimal. Since there is nothing special about the ContactUsPage class, it can inherit all of the interactions from the Page super class. But what if we wanted to implement a HomePage class?

The majority of the pages on our website follow the same four section layout described in the *Describing a web page with objects* section of this chapter. However, the home page has six major sections, as shown in the following image:

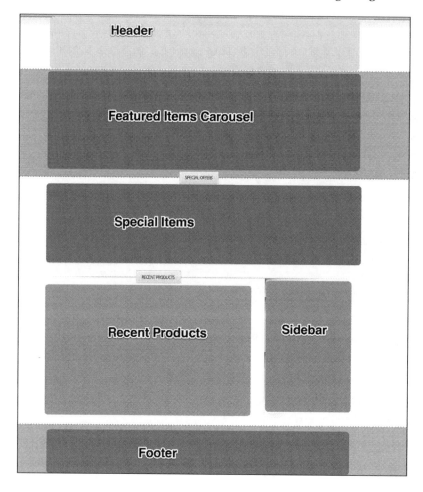

The `body` section of the page is missing; it with Featured Items Carousel, the **Special Items** section, and the **Recent Products** section. The **Header**, **Sidebar**, and **Footer** sections remain the same. So the `HomePage` class needs to reflect this uniqueness. Let's take a look at the `class` definition:

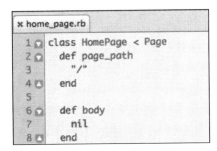

```ruby
class HomePage < Page
  def page_path
    "/"
  end

  def body
    nil
  end
```

We start the class by declaring the path of the existing page, so that the `verify` method can check that we are on the right page. Also, we overwrite the `body` method from the super class. Since the home page does not technically have a main body section, we will just return a `nil`. Next, we will implement the three methods needed to access the unique page sections found on the home page.

```ruby
def special_items
  @selenium.find_elements(:class, "special-item").collect do |element|
    SpecialItem.new(element, @selenium)
  end
end

def featured_item_carousel
  #Implement me
end

def recent_products
  #Implement me
end
```

On line **10**, we have a method that searches for all instances of the `special-item` class and creates an array of the `SpecialItem` objects. Since we do not have a test that uses the `featured_item_carousel` or `recent_products` sections, we will not implement these methods yet. However, we will have a test that will add one of the **Special Offers** item to the cart, so let's take a quick look at the `SpecialItem` class:

```ruby
class SpecialItem
    def initialize(element, selenium)
        @element = element
        @selenium = selenium
    end

    def add_to_cart
        @element.find_element(:class, "add-to-cart").click
        @selenium.find_element(:id, "fancybox-outer").find_element(:class, "purAddToCart").click
    end
end
```

Each `SpecialItem` object initializes with the `element` that WebDriver found on the home page. This is done so that each `SpecialItem` instance has a reference only to itself, that is, it does not know about the existence of other special items on the home page. Furthermore, each `SpecialItem` object implements an `add_to_cart` method as an action that it can perform.

Note that the reference to `selenium` is passed into the `SpecialItem` class. Typically, having the `element` reference alone is not only enough but is encouraged since we want the class to be as isolated as possible. However, due to peculiarities of our website's implementation, after clicking on the **Add To Cart** button for a product, a review modal opens up. This is shown in the following screenshot:

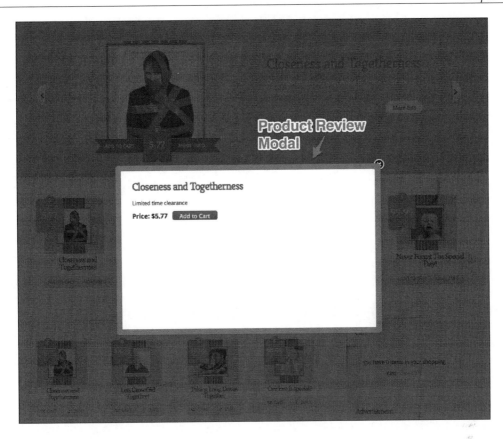

The modal does not reside within the scope of the `SpecialItem` object, so we need access to the whole scope of the page to add the item to the cart. This workaround is atypical.

 Whenever possible, make each Page Object element as *dumb and blind* of anything else happening on the page as possible. The less they know about the world outside of them, the easier it is to maintain them in the long run.

After adding the `SpecialItems` object to the `HomePage` class, our test should easily be able to add a product to the cart with this simple to understand line of code:

```
HomePage.new(@selenium).special_items.first.add_to_cart
```

The preceding method call will add the `first` product in the **Special Offers** section to the cart. We can add more functionality to the `SpecialItem` class as necessary. For example, instead of choosing the item to add by the position in the array, such as `first` or `third`, we can add a method to select the desired `SpecialItem` object by product `name` or by target URL. Our test might look like this:

```
HomePage.new(@selenium).special_items.find("Our love is special!!").
add_to_cart
```

We will not go into the implementation details of this functionality, but it sounds like a worthy exercise for the reader to practice with. Last but not least, let's put together all of the code we just added into a test!

Increasing the number of sidebar objects as the website grows

Before moving on to implementations of Page Objects in different testing frameworks, let's think about our `SidebarCart` class and how it will organically change as our website changes. Let's start by adding new methods to test the existing functionality.

When writing a test that checks individual items in our cart, for things such as quantity or unit price, all we have to do is add a couple of new methods to retrieve this information. We can also add a couple of methods that will perform an action of clicking on the **View Cart** and **Checkout** links:

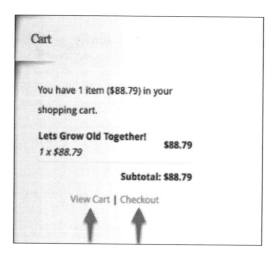

These methods will allow us to interact with specific parts of the web page. If in the future our website adds functionality to modify the contents of the cart from the sidebar, such as changing quantity or deleting items, we can easily add two new methods to accomplish this as well. Once the initial framework is set up, the functionality added to it will grow organically as the test needs change.

Running tests with the Page Objects framework

The largest advantage of the Page Object pattern is that it is not a zero-sum approach. That is, we do not need to convert the entire test suite to the Page Object framework to take advantage of it. Instead, we can slowly add new `Page` subclasses as they are needed and updating the existing tests to use the newly created classes as they become available. For a while, our test suite might look like a hybrid of direct Selenium `click` methods and the `add_to_cart` methods from the framework. This is perfectly acceptable as long as our code is continuously improving in the positive direction.

> In the following test examples, we are not using the *The Action Wrapper pattern* section from *Chapter 5, Stabilizing the Tests*. Thus, we have a mix of Selenium `get` and `click` method calls, and we are missing all of the stability improvements added in that chapter. This is done for both brevity and to demonstrate that the test suite can be improved in small portions.

Using Page Objects in the Test::Unit framework

The Test::Unit framework that we have been using since *Chapter 1, Writing the First Test*, is a good starting point to implement our Page Objects. The test, minus the `setup` and `teardown` methods, will look like this:

```ruby
12
13    def test_cart_on_contact_page
14      @selenium.get "http://awful-valentine.com/"
15
16      page = HomePage.new(@selenium)
17      page.special_items.first.add_to_cart
18      @selenium.get "http://awful-valentine.com/contact-us"
19
20      page = ContactUsPage.new(@selenium)
21      assert_equal("You have 1 item ($5.77) in your shopping cart.",
22                   page.sidebar.cart.summary)
23      assert_equal("$5.77", page.sidebar.cart.subtotal)
24    end
25
```

After navigating to the home page on line **14**, we allow the HomePage object take over the test. Using this Page object, we add an item to the cart and then navigate to the **Contact Us** page on line **18**. On line **20**, the ContactUsPage object takes over and validates that we have landed on the appropriate web page, as all of the Page subclasses do. We then use the method chain to retrieve the summary and subtotal of the shopping cart.

As you can see, with this method, our test knows very little about the classes and IDs of different elements on the page. This may seem excessive and complicated at first; after all, when writing our test in Selenium, we want to be able to click on buttons from within the test. However, the possibilities that open up to us when using this approach are endless. Let's take a look at this piece of code in particular:

```
ContactUsPage.new(@selenium).sidebar.cart.summary
```

This code explains to us the behavior of our application in just a few simple method names. From this, we know the following facts about the current page:

- Our test should be on the **Contact Us** page, represented by the ContactUsPage object.

- The **Contact Us** page has a concept of sidebar, unlike some pages that do not. The SideBar object will allow us to interact with items within.

- We know that within the current page's sidebar, we can find a shopping cart, and use the SidebarCart object to interact with it.

- With the use of the SidebarCart object, we can retrieve summary of the cart or the subtotal.

We get all of this information by just looking at the method call, isn't that amazing? If we wanted to implement a method that retrieves the shopping cart summary by using Selenium alone, our code would look like this:

```
@selenium.find_element(:id, "sidebar")
        .find_element(:class, "widget")
        .find_element(:id, "Cart66AdvancedSidebarAjax")
        .find_element(:id, "Cart66WidgetCartEmptyAdvanced").text
```

The test now has all of the IDs and classes hard coded in it. Furthermore, if we change the plugin we are using to display our sidebar cart, these IDs and classes will change. We will have to fix every instance it is used. With the Page Object pattern, the only change that we will need to make in our framework is how the Sidebar and SidebarCart classes locate the web elements on the page. Since the code is stored in a central place, all of the tests will automatically start using the new implementation of our website.

Let's run our Test::Unit test and make sure that it is passing with our test framework:

```
mbp-3:code dima$ ruby test_unit_example.rb
Run options:

# Running tests:

.

Finished tests in 11.802721s, 0.0847 tests/s, 0.1695 assertions/s.

1 tests, 2 assertions, 0 failures, 0 errors, 0 skips
```

The new test is working great! Let's take a look at how the test would be implemented in RSpec and Cucumber.

Using Page Objects in different testing frameworks

Our framework is independent from different testing tools. This means that we can use it with Test::Unit, Cucumber, and RSpec tools, but it is not limited to just them. This is great for us, since it allows us to follow the test tool independence pattern, which we will discuss in greater detail in the next section. In the meantime, let's pretend that we have a large website with multiple teams working on different sections of the website. As always, some teams will want to test the code with the tools they are comfortable with. The good news is that everyone can test the entire website using the tool of their choosing, while at the same time, sharing the framework code.

Looking at the Cucumber implementation

Since we have used Cucumber extensively in *Chapter 6, Testing the Behavior*, let's start with it. The team responsible for implementing the sidebar widgets, such as the cart, loves to test with Cucumber. They have written this feature definition:

```
cucumber_example.feature ×
1   Feature: sidebar cart should display correct information on all pages.
2
3
4   Scenario: User adds checks sidebar cart on contact us page
5     Given I am on the home page
6     And I add first special offers item to the cart
7
8     And I navigate to Contact Us Page
9     Then the shopping cart should have correct information
10
11
```

To implement this test, we will have the following step definitions:

```
1
2  Given(/^I am on the home page$/) do
3    @selenium = Selenium::WebDriver.for(:firefox)
4    @selenium.get "http://awful-valentine.com/"
5  end
6
7  Given(/^I add first special offers item to the cart$/) do
8    page = HomePage.new(@selenium)
9    page.special_items.first.add_to_cart
10 end
11
12 Given(/^I navigate to Contact Us Page$/) do
13    @selenium.get "http://awful-valentine.com/contact-us"
14 end
15
16 Then(/^the shopping cart should have correct information$/) do
17    page = ContactUsPage.new(@selenium)
18    expect(page.sidebar.cart.summary).to eq("You have 1 item ($5.77) in your shopping cart.")
19    expect(page.sidebar.cart.subtotal).to eq("$5.77")
20    @selenium.quit
21 end
```

As we can see, aside from a slightly different way of declaring steps, the interaction with different pages remains the same. The consistency in how the tests interact with the web pages is very important, because it allows different teams understand the tests written by another team with another tool. Let's run our Cucumber test and make sure it passes:

```
mbp-3:code dima$ cucumber -r page_objects/cucumber_steps.rb cucumber_example.feature
Feature: sidebar cart should display correct information on all pages.

  Scenario: User adds checks sidebar cart on contact us page # cucumber_example.feature:4
    Given I am on the home page                              # page_objects/cucumber_steps.rb:5
    And I add first special offers item to the cart          # page_objects/cucumber_steps.rb:10
    And I navigate to Contact Us Page                        # page_objects/cucumber_steps.rb:15
    Then the shopping cart should have correct information    # page_objects/cucumber_steps.rb:19

1 scenario (1 passed)
4 steps (4 passed)
0m11.556s
```

Looking at the RSpec implementation

RSpec is a BDD tool that follows a similar philosophy as Cucumber: *test the behavior of the application, not the implementation*. RSpec uses a different syntax to accomplish this task. Unlike Cucumber, which tries to describe the behavior in a human language, RSpec tries to use a much more rigid syntax that does not allow as much variation in how someone can describe functionality. Since RSpec definitions resemble a programming language instead of the human language, some developers prefer it to Cucumber.

> Even though both RSpec and Cucumber are great tools for testing behavior, the minor difference between them cause a lot of strife between some developers. These debates of preference remind me of Mac versus Windows versus Linux arguments typically heard on any development team.

The team responsible for the shopping cart functionality loves to write tests using RSpec or Test::Unit. To test the shopping cart in the sidebar widget, we will write a test like this:

```
2
3   describe "Sidebar Shopping cart" do
4     context "contact us page" do
5
6       before(:all) do
7         @selenium = Selenium::WebDriver.for(:firefox)
8       end
9
10      after(:all) do
11        @selenium.quit
12      end
13
14      it "should have correct subtotal and summary" do
15        @selenium.get "http://awful-valentine.com/"
16
17        page = HomePage.new(@selenium)
18        page.special_items.first.add_to_cart
19        @selenium.get "http://awful-valentine.com/contact-us"
20
21        page = ContactUsPage.new(@selenium)
22        expect(page.sidebar.cart.summary).to eq("You have 1 item ($5.77) in your shopping cart.")
23        expect(page.sidebar.cart.subtotal).to eq("$5.77")
24      end
25    end
```

As we can see, some things are slightly different from everything we have written so far. The before and after methods take the place of setup and teardown, and the description of the functionality is made in short clipped describe, context, and it statements. The interactions with the page, however, remain the same between the three tools. Let's run the RSpec test to make sure everything is passing:

```
mbp-3:code dima$ rspec rspec_example.rb
.

Finished in 11.85 seconds (files took 0.4129 seconds to load)
1 example, 0 failures
```

Now that we have working examples of it, let's formally define the test tool independence pattern.

The test tool independence pattern

Test tool independence occurs when the test suite is not heavily integrated with any given testing tool. For example, switching from Selenium 1 to Selenium WebDriver is difficult, because both tools use different methods to locate and click on page elements. If we wrote our framework in such a way as to hide these changing methods from the test, all we need to do to upgrade to Selenium WebDriver is update the find_element and click methods to use the new WebDriver API. This practice is referred to as the Adapter pattern. In the previous example of this chapter, the SidebarCart class acts as an adapter between the test and the instance of Selenium WebDriver by translating the add_to_cart method call into a WebDriver click method.

 In software design, Adapter pattern is used to map functionality of different objects that have different interfaces. Adding an adapter object between the two objects that wish to communicate with each other does this; the adapter object acts as an interpreter between the two objects.

Just because our test suite is written with the Page Object pattern does not make it test tool independent. It is just as easy to lock into a given tool or a specific version of that tool inside of a Page class.

Advantages of the test tool independence

There are many advantages of writing our test framework in such a way that it does not directly depend on any testing tool. Let's look at several of these here:

- **Easy upgrade**: Different tools, such as gems or libraries, change all the time. As new features are added, the public methods might change completely, becoming incompatible with previous versions. By hiding the method implementation from the test, our test does not need to know about the current version of any third-party library.

- **Easy tool switching**: With our framework, we can switch between the testing tools we want without chaining the test core much. This applies both to testing frameworks, such as Cucumber, but also applies to the testing tool, such as Selenium. After all, just because our tests are written in a regular Firefox browser today, it does not mean we will not want to add support for Chrome or a headless browser in the future.

- **Consistent descriptive API**: Since our framework describes behavior, such as adding item to the cart, instead of listing a series of clicks required to accomplish that task, it is easy to read and understand our test's intention.

Disadvantages of the test tool independence

As always, every time we make our test more independent and resilient, we increase the amount of complexity and overhead. A simple test, described earlier in the chapter, can be written in a few lines of code if we allow the test to talk directly to Selenium. With the intention of making our test suite future-proof, we have to add many new wrapper and adapter classes today.

The right way to implement Page Objects

I will not venture a claim that the implementation of the Page Objects in this chapter is the right and only way to do it. Just like there are many programming languages and different ways to write code, there are multiple ways to implement Page Objects. Choosing the right approach will be one of the first and most difficult tasks to figure out. I'd like to spend this section talking about different approaches we could have taken when writing our framework.

Making pages smarter than tests

In the framework we implemented, the @selenium instance is passed between different Page objects as the test progresses. For example, after we have created an instance of Firefox browser with WebDriver, we pass it into each class like this:

```
@selenium.get "http://awful-valentine.com/"
page = HomePage.new(@selenium)
page.special_items.first.add_to_cart

ShoppingCartPage.new(@selenium)
```

This approach is good because it is clear to see the order of progression from page to page. It's clear to see that @selenium moves first to the home page and hands off itself to the HomePage object. Then, the test adds a product into the shopping cart, followed by test's expectation that the ShoppingCartPage class will be needed next. In this scenario, the test is smart and the pages are dumb. If we make our pages smarter and the test dumber, our code will look like this:

```
@selenium.get "http://awful-valentine.com/"
page = HomePage.new(@selenium)
page.special_items.first.add_to_cart
assert_equal("$5.77", page.cart.total)
```

In the preceding code, the ShoppingCartPage object is never explicitly declared, so the test is oblivious to the class it is asserting against. All it knows is that the next page will contain a shopping cart object that will return a total value.

The implementation of the add_to_cart method in the SpecialItem class will change to become smarter. This is the code from before the change:

```
def add_to_cart
  @element.find_element(:class, "add-to-cart").click
  @selenium.find_element(:id, "fancybox-outer").find_element(:class, "purAddToCart").click
end
```

Now, this method will know that `ShoppingCartPage` is the next in the application flow, and it will return that object back to the test:

```
def add_to_cart
  @element.find_element(:class, "add-to-cart").click
  @selenium.find_element(:id, "fancybox-outer").find_element(:class, "purAddToCart").click
  ShoppingCartPage.new(@selenium)
end
```

The instance of `@selenium` is passed between the objects. We can take this approach further and make the test not use `@selenium` at all. In the following code, the test no longer knows the URL of the `HomePage`, because the `HomePage` class has a new `navigate_to` method that takes care of navigation:

```
@selenium = Selenium::WebDriver.for(:firefox)
page = HomePage.new(@selenium).navigate_to
```

With this approach, the test dictates what needs to be done, while the test framework takes care of how things should be done. One thing to be careful about is that the framework will become too smart, that is, the behavior logic is stored in the framework and not in the test. See the *Placing logic in Page Objects* section for more information.

Making tests smarter than pages

We can head in the opposite direction and make the tests know how the application should behave, while leaving as little logic in the `Page` classes as possible. One way to accomplish this is to make all of the page interactions into static class methods. Our test code will look something like this:

```
@selenium = Selenium::WebDriver.for(:firefox)
HomePage.special_items(@selenium).first.add_to_cart
ShoppingCartPage.cart(@selenium).total
```

Now our pages are stateless, that is, every time we want to perform an action, we have to pass in the current instance of `@selenium` to it. The test is the one that dictates the flow of the application, and the `Page` classes only perform the actions they are requested to only with the information provided by the test.

Which should be smarter, the test or the page? That's a tough question, probably the best solution is to have a compromise and make parts of the Page Object framework smart and other parts intentionally dumb, as the situation dictates.

Using modules instead of inheritance

When I first learned about object inheritance, I wanted to use it everywhere. This is typical of any new skill or programming pattern we learn as developers. However, sometimes a module/mixin is a better and cleaner solution than creating an inheritance hierarchy. In the framework we created, we used inheritance to give different pages ability to access the header, footer, and other objects on the page. This setup works well if most of the web pages on our website are extremely similar. In case of the HomePage class, we had to overwrite the body method because the home page didn't have that section.

This approach will quickly become complicated if we have to overwrite nonexisting objects on every new Page subclass we create. Instead of inheriting everything from the Page superclass, a more practical solution would be to have each individual subpage import only the functionality it has and ignore everything that does not apply.

Placing logic in Page Objects

One of the useful shortcuts we added in the Page class is the verify method. Each page automatically checks itself to make sure it is where it is supposed to be. We can add more logic to verify that the page is completely loaded. For example, if we have a certain image or form that needs to appear on the page every time, we could make that check happen automatically the page loads the page. If for whatever reason the element is not present, the test will fail, saying that the page was not completely loaded.

It is too easy to get carried away with verifying everything. Having some verification can be useful in debugging a test failure, but putting too much logic into the Page classes can be detrimental in the long term. Let's take a look at two scenarios where we have too much logic in our Page Object:

- Every page class contains detailed information about all the elements on the page. If the social network icons are missing or some content such as an image is missing, the Page Object framework throws an error to let us know that the page is not fully loaded. This is good practice when testing for page completeness every time; however, it might prevent a registration test from completing because an unrelated asset is missing.

- The login action on the Page Object checks whether the browser already has a logged in user. This check will log out the current user and login with the user the test desires. This useful check can prevent test failures due to data pollution from previous tests, where the previous test did not teardown properly. At the same time, this functionality can mask a poorly written test, which reduces the quality and usefulness of the test suite as a whole.

In conclusion, be wary about putting too much logic into the individual Page classes.

Summary

In this chapter, you had a brief introduction to the Page Object pattern. Using this pattern, we are able to create a test suite framework, which is simple to understand and easy to maintain in the long term. We discussed different advantages of using the Page Objects as opposed to writing direct Selenium commands. These advantages are portability, upgradability, and reusability.

By using the test tool independence pattern, we demonstrated that our Page Object framework could be used with any testing tool the development wishes to use. We concluded the chapter by discussing several alternative implementations for the framework.

In the next chapter, we will talk about prioritizing the test growth in the test suite. We will also discuss different ways to manage our test environments.

8

Growing the Test Suite

"To succeed, planning alone is insufficient. One must improvise as well."

-Isaac Asimov, Foundation Series

Writing tests is fun! This may seem contrary to the first sentence in *Chapter 1, Writing the First Test*, of this book. However, once we solve the difficult problems such as test stability, test data, and the framework design, writing a new test case is the most gratifying experience one can have in our field.

Once we have a good grasp of Selenium and are ready to grow our test suite, we will face some new challenges. Questions such as what test needs to be written next or what CI tool to choose from will naturally come up. In this chapter, we will discuss the following topics about the long-term growth and maintenance of the test suite:

- Strategies for writing test suites
- Different types of tests
- Different types of test suites
- Continuous Integration
- Testing in multiple browsers
- Selenium Grid
- Managing build nodes
- Build node virtualization
- Frequently Asked Questions

Strategies for writing test suites

A common question during a job interview for test automation is "How do you plan to build the test suite?" When I was new to software test automation, I would answer that 99 percent coverage is critical. After reality had a chance to catch up, it became apparent that such high coverage is impossible due to obvious time constraints.

Instead of having 100 percent test coverage, the best that can be done is to prioritize the growth of the test suites. In this section, we will discuss the order in which test suits should be built. As we build our test suites, some tests will cross multiple boundaries, which is perfectly normal. However, it is best to have a way to group certain tests together so they can be executed individually. For example the smoke test suite is a subset of the regression suite, but we need ability to execute it without having to run the regression suite.

[All of the strategies listed are in order from highest priority to lowest, but they are not mutually exclusive.]

Different types of tests

Before we dive into the different Selenium test suites, let's define several types of automated tests. This will help us understand where Selenium tests belong in the development cycle. The following definitions are commonly used to describe a type of an individual test; however, they are slightly redefined with Selenium bias:

- **Unit test**: This is, by definition, the smallest test unit. This type of a test is written to test an individual object and even individual methods of said object. Unit testing is highly important because it prevents bugs from creeping in at the lowest level. These tests rarely use any production-like test data and often solely rely on mock data. Since unit tests are at a low level of the application, Selenium tests are not applicable here.

[Low level is a phrase commonly used to describe code that has a low level of abstraction. Likewise, high level describes code with a high level of abstraction. For example, a method that adds 1 and 1 would be described as low level and a method that registers a new user in the database is a high-level method.]

- **Integration test**: This consists of several modules of code put together, allowing them to pass data between each other. The purpose of this type of test is to make sure that all modules integrate and work with each other. In terms of Selenium, integration might be checking that the store module of our website can pass the product information into the cart module. The tests that run in CI after every commit to test only our application and stubbing all third-party services is considered integration build.

Integration tests are sometimes referred to as functional tests, since they test the functionality of an application.

- **End-to-end**: This is the highest-level of test. This type of test is executed in production or a production-like environment, such as staging. Similar to integration tests, an end-to-end test tries to verify that all of the components, including third-party services, can communicate well with each other.

End-to-end tests are sometimes referred to as **Verification and Validation (V&V)**

The majority of Selenium tests will fall into the integration category. By blocking as much instability caused by test data and third-party dependencies as possible, our tests can concentrate on testing only one piece of functionality at the time. However, a well-written test that is properly hermetically sealed should be able to run in both integration and end-to-end environments.

See *Hermetic Test Pattern* in *Chapter 3, Refactoring Tests*, for more information.

The smoke test suite

Smoke testing is a very common and popular concept in the quality assurance world. The idea is to plug in the new code, let it run, and see whether it runs or catches on fire. Out of all the test suites, a smoke suite will by far be the smallest in size, since it needs to give a close to instantaneous pass or fail verdict. This test suite is best used in the first few minutes after new code is deployed to any environment. Use this small test suite to make sure that the production environment is up and running.

Tests in the smoke test suite should look for the following:

- **Running application**: Does the website load or does it give a 500 error? This is by far the simplest question and could be answered by navigating to several key pages, such as the home page or the online store.

- **Database connection**: Database issues happen more often than anyone cares to admit. After the deployment of the new code, we realize that the database was not properly migrated. Test should do several *read only* checks against the database, such as log in with an existing user.

- **Abnormal amount of exception**: This question is a little bit more involving than others. The starting point is to make sure no page returns an error code when it should not. It can evolve into dumping the JavaScript console logs to check whether new JavaScript errors start to appear.

Smoke test suite should almost be like a feather in a boxing fight. It should touch the application without leaving a single dent or scratch. We should keep the following in mind:

- **Avoid writing to a database if you cannot clean it up after**: It is normal to register new users or make purchases on a staging environment. However, this is typically a bad idea in production, since it is difficult to clean up the test data after the test is complete. To stay on the safe side, the test should only perform actions that read from the database, never write to it.

- **Don't test too much**: We want to have an answer about the state of the environment as fast as possible. Leave the more extensive testing to other test suites.

The money path suite

Money path is one or several core key pathway through our application. In the case of an online store, it is the ability to add items to the cart and receive payment information. In an inventory management system, it's the ability to retrieve and update current inventory. Noncritical functionality, such as updating user's email preferences, is to be left out of this test suite.

Money path and smoke test strategies can have multiple tests in common; however, tests that write to the database in the money path suite should probably not be included in the Smoke Test suite.

The money path suite should answer the following question: is the customer prevented from giving us money? This is by far the most important part of this suite. Every single test in this test suite should aim to answer that question, if it's not it should be moved to another test suite.

New feature growth strategy

Smoke test suite and money path suites are the top priority when writing tests. However, those test suites are relatively small and will go into maintenance mode pretty quickly. After they are finished, we will spend the majority of our time in this mode. The idea of the new feature strategy is to keep up with the development of the application. As a new feature is added, we add a new test. This strategy does not try to write tests for an already existing functionality such as regression strategy.

By far, this new feature strategy is most effective when the test writer is embedded in the development team.

Some of the teams I've personally worked on, the developers themselves were responsible for the creation of new tests as the application got new features. This gave an up-to-date Selenium test support for all new features and gave the QA team a starting point to add and improve the said tests. This setup has been extremely successful.

Being part of the team on a daily basis and seeing the direction of development is an important part in keeping up with new features. The classic over-the-wall approach to quality assurance will not work well because by the time the test developer starts writing tests for newly delivered feature, the development team has moved on to new tasks.

The over-the-wall testing approach consists of the Development and QA teams being completely separate. After a new set of features has been added to the application, the new build is given to the QA team to test. The QA members are not involved in daily testing as each commit happens.

When writing tests for new features, the tests should concentrate on answering the following questions:

- Is this the most important and critical feature to be tested?

    There are new features that enhance the application slightly and there are critical features. When pressed for time, as we always are, the new tests should aim to test mission critical features and leave the enhancements to the regression suite.

- Are the new tests useful right away?

    As soon as a new test is written, even for an unfinished feature, it should be added to CI. Features that are in active development have the maximum instances of instability and bugs by far. Having the new tests added in step with new code and running on every commit provides a good foundation for stability.

Bug-driven growth strategy

Bug-driven and new feature strategies are extremely compatible with each other. The new feature strategy concentrates on adding a new test for every new feature. The bug-driven strategy concentrates on adding a new test for every bug discovered and fixed.

Every new release of the application comes with a list of new features or bug fixes, and more often than not, both at the same time. Most people who will be testing the new release of the application will concentrate on testing the new features, while giving the bug fixes a cursory glance. Having an automated test case for every bug fixed in the current build is a great safety net. Furthermore, sometimes when a new release branch is being created in the **Version Control System (VCS)**, bug fixes are sometimes overwritten or reverted by accident. A single test might prevent an emergency deploy!

 An accidental revert of a bug fix may not be the most common occurrence on a team familiar with their VCS tool; when it does happen, it happens at the worst possible time.

The regression suite

Regression tests are all of the tests in our suite that test features developed in the past; this is not to be confused with features actively being developed. Following the previously-described strategies, we will add new tests to the regression test suite.

Sadly, more often than not, our teams will always be too understaffed to write new tests against already existing features. When pressed for time, we should always concentrate on new features, since this part of the code will prove to be most unstable. As new bugs are discovered in older code and feature set, the regression suite will slowly grow. However, spending too much time writing tests for sections of code that were not touched in years will probably prove to be a waste of time.

The 99 percent coverage suite

A test suite that covers 99 percent of new and existing features in an application is the dream of every tester. However, it often proves to be nothing but a pipe dream. Unless we are on the team writing tests for the space station or a nuclear power plant, we will never have enough resources to test everything. Thus, for most automated test creators, this strategy is not only wasteful but can be extremely harmful.

Any piece of the application that has not been touched in a long time and has not had any bugs in that time is unlikely to randomly start producing bugs. Writing a test for that code may be harmful because it takes time away from writing a test for new code that more than likely will break. However, if the said old code starts to be updated with a bug fix or a new feature, it's a good idea to write tests for it.

On the other hand, if you are in a very fortunate position where you can afford to keep updating the test suite, bringing it closer and closer to full coverage, consider yourself extremely lucky and keep going!

One last thought about adding new tests to our application before we move on, is that it is always better to have a smaller test suite that is reliable and is executed often, than to have a large test suite that fails randomly and makes everyone on the team lose faith in its usefulness.

> As soon as we start to add any test to our suite, it's a good time to start thinking about CI.

Continuous Integration

The most amazing test suite ever written is useless if it sits on someone's laptop and is never executed! Having our tests in CI is not only beneficial to the quality of the application, but it is also beneficial to the quality of the test suite itself. By executing the test suite dozens of times a day we can discover test instabilities, which occur once in a while.

There are five components to setting up a Continuous Integration system. They are listed in order of importance here:

- **Test environment**: In order to execute the tests, we need to have an application we are trying to test. Without a test environment, the tests are just pieces of code that cannot be executed. We talked about different types of test environments in the *Data relevance versus data accessibility* section of *Chapter 4, Data-driven Testing*.

> Even if it is possible to execute a more complicated test suite than a smoke test in a production environment, it is an anti-pattern that should be avoided.

- **Test data**: Having access to reliable test data is very important. After all, the test's only role is to pass data from one location in our application to another and check the outcome. We discussed the Test Data problems and solutions in *Chapter 4, Data-driven Testing*.

- **Tests and test stability**: Developing the test suite the next item on the list. We discussed some strategies on prioritizing the order of the tests earlier in this chapter. Remember, do not let the pace of test suite growth reduce the quality of individual tests and the test suite as a whole. We discussed improving test stability and reliability in *Chapter 5, Stabilizing the Tests*.

- **Test nodes**: Managing the computers that host the test environment and the testing nodes is important. Having a stable application and test suite can be completely negated by a test environment, which randomly deletes the database or test nodes that restart at will. We will cover these issues further in the *Managing the test environments and nodes* section.

- **CI system**: Choosing the right CI tool seems like the top priority; how can we execute our tests without it? However, if the preceding four points are properly resolved, the tool that executes the tests can be completely interchangeable; thus, it is the least important item on our list. We will talk more about choosing the right CI tool in the *Choosing the CI tool* section.

 The statement made in this bullet can only remain true if the investment made into the current CI tool is minimal. We will discuss some ways to reduce dependency on a specific CI tool in the *Choosing the CI tool* section.

Managing the test environments and nodes

The management of CI and testing environments is often ignored. The development team is often too busy or doesn't want to play the role of a systems administrator. The production system administrators might be able to help with managing the hardware and the operating system of staging and testing environments, but making dozens of deployments of new code to those environments can become taxing on them.

For these reasons, the quality assurance and test automation teams must fill in that role. They are the ones who care the most about these environments and having a more intimate knowledge of how the application is deployed can provide a lot of insight on why certain bugs occur; not to mention a more detailed bug report, for which all of the developers are eternally grateful! There are two aspects of environment management that naturally fall into this field: the testing environment and the CI environment.

Deploying new builds

Being able to reliably deploy new code into a testing environment at the drop of a hat is extremely useful both for manual and automated testing. Testing new features or verifying that a bug is fixed as soon as the new build released is great for a fast feedback cycle and reduction in frustration for all parties involved.

Luckily for us, we do not necessarily have to do a lot of work to make this a reality. Most of the time, the production operations administrators have scripts written to help them deploy new versions. By working with those teams, it is possible to get a hold of those scripts and adopt them to work with Integration and Staging testing environments. Combining those deployments scripts with CI build, we are able to deploy the latest build into our test environment and automatically trigger a Selenium smoke test suite. Depending on the test environment, we even are able to run the whole regression test suite.

We do not necessarily need to have system administrator experience to have the tools to make our day-to-day life easier. Convincing all parties involved that a QA team, which is independent, is a huge time and money saver. Very few people can argue against that logic.

CI environment management

Managing the CI environment can be slightly more involved compared to having deployment scripts to a testing environment. We need to manage the build nodes, the test data, and the scripts to execute the test build. There is a lot of work to do in this area, but keeping these items stable will prevent a lot of flakey builds. Let's talk about node management first.

Build node management

Whether we are talking about CI build nodes or Selenium Grid nodes, in an ideal world, all of them would be identical to each other. Having the same version of all tools and environment settings, such as the version of Java or the same version of Firefox, will prevent failures that cannot be easily replicated or explained. There are several ways to approach this problem:

- Configuration Management System
- Virtualization

Configuration management system

There are several commercial and open source configuration management systems available. These tools take care of managing third-party applications, dependencies, and configurations on large quantities of computers. These tools will not only help you manage the testing nodes, but will also help you to manage the computers used by both development and testing teams. Having all of the environments in sync with production will prevent odd surprises once the code is deployed for the customers.

Early on in my career, I was a manual and automated tester on a Java-based web project. When the whole website overhaul effort was completed and deployed to production, we noticed some poor performance and strange bugs that were never seen in testing environments. After further inspection, it was discovered that the version of Java used on production severs was one minor version behind from development and testing environment. The difference caused a forced rollback and delay of this major undertaking, not to mention embarrassment for the whole team involved.

After learning this valuable lesson, it has always been my priority to manage all of the build nodes properly. Here are the tools that I was able to use successfully in the past to avoid instability:

- **Chef**: This is a Ruby cross-platform tool that allows you to group computers on your network into groups and assign which applications and versions of said applications are to be installed on per-group basis. Find more information about Chef at `http://www.getchef.com/chef/`.

- **Puppet**: This is a Ruby-based configuration management, which is a direct competitor to Chef. Both have an analogous feature set; you can find more information about Puppet at `http://puppetlabs.com/`.

- **Shell scripts**: When you do not have ability to use a full configuration management system, having some shell scripts is drastically better than trying to manage each node by hand. You can use Bash scripts on Linux-based systems and batch and PowerShell scripts on Windows-based systems. Having a script that downloads, installs the correct tools, and manages the configuration of the operating system is a worthwhile initial investment that will pay off in the long run.

 If you wish to use Bash scripts on a Windows node instead of writing it as a batch or PowerShell file, installing Cygwin is a great solution. Cygwin can be found at `https://www.cygwin.com/install.html`.

Virtualization

Virtualization is another way to manage build nodes. It can be combined with a configuration management system or by itself. By setting up a base **Virtual Machine (VM)** image of a testing node, we can configure an environment to be optimal for testing. After the base image has been created, we can copy it to create as many nodes as necessary without spending any time in configuring individual ones. Furthermore, VMs are great for periodically deleting the whole OS and starting again from an optimal environment!

There are dozens of free and enterprise VM solutions available on the market. Each comes with its own feature set and some might work much better for your individual situation than others. Here are several free virtualization solutions:

- **Xen project**: This is an open source virtualization product that allows users to host multiple concurrent VMs. This allows users to host both Linux-and Windows-based VMs. This is a lightweight, highly stable and highly reliable solution to host multiple simple build nodes. The biggest drawback of Xen is that it can only be hosted on a Linux-based host computer, and requires some system administrator skills; simply put, it is not overly user friendly. More information about Xen project can be found at `http://www.xenproject.org`.

- **Virtual box**: This is an open source project by Oracle. It runs on many host operating systems such as Windows, Linux, and Mac OSX. Virtual Box supports many types of guest VMs, such as Windows, Linux, and Mac OSX. Virtual box is user friendly and easy to get started with. More information on virtual box can be found at `https://www.virtualbox.org`.

- **Windows virtual PC**: This is a free VM host provided by Microsoft. This can only be run on a Windows host, and have only provided Windows guest VMs. For more information about Windows virtual PC, please refer to `http://www.microsoft.com/windows/virtual-pc/`.

Selenium Grid

While we are on the topic of build nodes, let's briefly visit Selenium Grid. So far, we have been writing our tests and executing them only on our local computers. This type of test execution is called the standalone mode of execution. The downside of standalone mode is that the resources available limit us on our current computer. For example, we can only use the browsers currently installed on the computer; basically, running your tests in Internet Explorer from a Mac is impossible. Selenium Grid solves these limitations by allowing our tests to take over other computers on our network. Thus, we are no longer limited by the resources on our computer, but can increase the coverage and reach of our test suite!

Understanding standalone and grid modes

To clear up any misconceptions on how Selenium Grid works, let's take a closer look at how WebDriver controls the web browser. Understanding the internal workings will help you set up a much more stable grid in the long run. Let's first take a look at how Selenium WebDriver controls a web browser with the JsonWire protocol.

JsonWire protocol

The JsonWire protocol (also known as the WebDriver Wire protocol) is a standard set of API calls that is used to communicate with the WebDriver server. Basically, when our test wants the browser to navigate to a certain page or click on a certain link, the language binding translates the `click` method call into the JsonWire protocol and sends it as an HTTP request to the WebDriver server.

 Detailed documentation on the JsonWire API can be found at `https://code.google.com/p/selenium/wiki/JsonWireProtocol`.

Since the JsonWire protocol is simple to understand and use, anyone can write a language binding to drive any browser!

 Throughout this book, we used Ruby bindings to control the browser; however, there's a binding for every major programming language. In some cases, there are multiple implementations of WebDriver bindings for a given programming language.

Standalone mode

When we run our Selenium tests in standalone mode, an instance of WebDriver server is started on our computer. This server controls the browser we are testing and we control the server through the language bindings. The following figure demonstrates the flow of commands from the test to the browser:

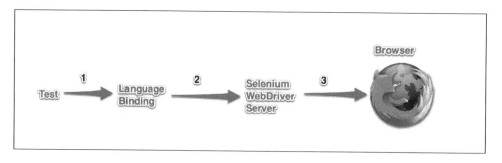

The `click` command follows these steps:

1. Our test finds the element it wants to click on and calls the `click` method.
2. The language binding, where the `click` method is defined, builds a simple JSON snippet. This snippet explains what action needs to be performed and what the target of the action is to the WebDriver server.
3. Selenium WebDriver server tells the web driver what action to perform.

Grid mode

Selenium Grid manages multiple computers, called nodes. Instead of connecting to a local instance of the Selenium WebDriver server, our tests connect to a central hub. The hub keeps track of all available nodes. The grid hub has the following responsibilities:

- Keep track of all available nodes
- Manage the creation and clean-up of test sessions
- Forward JsonWire communication between test bindings and nodes

When running tests using Selenium Grid, our tests are executed on a remote node in a remote browser, but everything acts as if we are running in standalone mode. The following diagram demonstrates how a `click` command works in the grid mode:

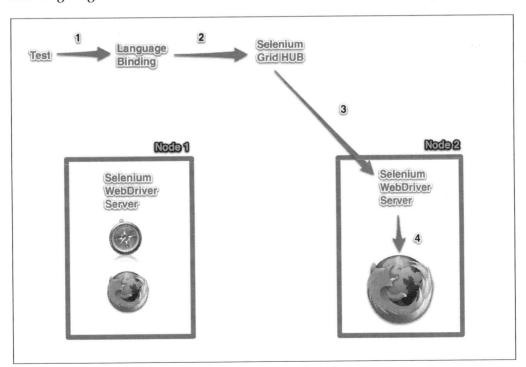

There are two things to note about the preceding diagram:

- As node 2 executes our tests, node 1 is idle; this means that we can start another test suite to run against node 1.

- Node 1 supports both the Firefox and Safari browsers. Our test suite can drive the Safari browser from any computer, even if that computer does not support Safari.

 SauceLabs is a company that set up a Grid-like infrastructure in the cloud. If you want to be able to test multiple browsers but do not have access or do not want to manage the grid nodes, they might be the right solution for you. Find more information at `https://saucelabs.com/`.

Installing Selenium Grid

Installing Selenium Grid on your network is as simple as finding several computers, downloading the Selenium WebDriver JAR file, and running the start command. If your IT department has several old computers that are out of date to be used in development but can still run at least one modern browser, you can build a large grid for your tests! Follow these steps to get started:

1. Download the latest version of the Selenium server from `http://docs.seleniumhq.org/download/`.

2. In the terminal, run the following command to start the Selenium hub (replacing PATH-TO-SELENIUM-JAR with the path to the downloaded JAR file):

   ```
   java -jar PATH-TO-SELENIUM-JAR.jar -role hub
   ```

   The terminal output should look something like this:

   ```
   : org.openqa.grid.selenium.GridLauncher main
   INFO: Launching a selenium grid server
   :INFO:osjs.Server:jetty-7.x.y-SNAPSHOT
   :INFO:osjsh.ContextHandler:started o.s.j.s.ServletContextHandler{/,null}
   :INFO:osjs.AbstractConnector:Started SocketConnector@0.0.0.0:4444
   ```

 This command is using all default settings, such as port number, for the hub to start on. To see all available settings, add the `-help` flag to the preceding command.

3. Now that the hub server has been started, let's add a node. In a new terminal window, run the following command:

```
java -jar PATH-TO-SELENIUM-JAR.jar -role wd -hub http://
localhost:4444 -port 5555
```

We added the -role wd flag to tell our JAR to start in WebDriver mode. The -hub flag is used to point the node to the hub location. Finally, the -port parameter is used to tell the node which port to listen on. The default port is 4444, which was occupied by the hub, so we use 5555 instead.

We have a small Selenium Grid up and running! Let's take a look at the grid console by navigating to http://localhost:4444/grid/console in our browser. We will see a summary of available nodes and browsers; it will look similar to this:

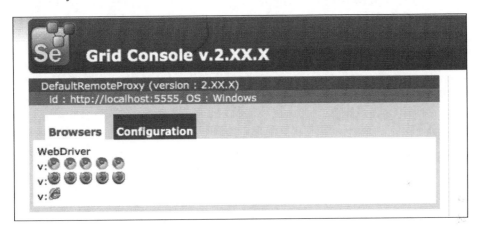

As we can see, our grid has one node that can run five instances of Chrome, five instances of Firefox, and one instance of Internet Explorer. Now that we have an active grid, we can point our tests at it.

Using Selenium Grid

It is very easy to start using our tests in grid mode. In *Chapter 1, Writing the First Test*, we used the following code to acquire a new instance of Firefox:

```
selenium = Selenium::WebDriver.for(:firefox)
```

By adding several new parameters to the WebDriver.for method call, we can request the new session to come from the Selenium Grid:

```
selenium = Selenium::WebDriver.for(:remote,
                                   :url => "http://localhost:4444",
                                   :desired_capabilities => :firefox)
```

The :remote parameter declares that the tests will run in Grid mode, and the Grid is located in the :url parameter. Finally, :desired_capabilities specifies the browser we want to use.

Selenium Grid Extras

Managing Selenium Grid can become quite involving. There are a lot of options and preferences for session management, timeouts, and much more. Selenium Grid can only control the web browsers on the nodes it manages. This means that someone has to manually manage all OS-level tasks on the Grid nodes. To help with the node management tasks, the Selenium Grid Extras project was created.

Selenium Grid Extras takes care of many aspects of grid management. Things such as automatically downloading new versions of WebDriver, periodically restarting the nodes, and viewing system resource usage can be handled by this project. To get more information about Selenium Grid Extras, please visit https://github.com/groupon/Selenium-Grid-Extras.

Whether we choose to use Selenium Grid for our testing in CI or not, we need to take environment maintenance seriously. In the next section, we will talk about managing both the test environments and the CI environments.

Choosing the CI tool

Since there are multiple open source and enterprise CI tools available on the market, the task of choosing one can be quite daunting. We can spend weeks comparing tables of features, licenses, capabilities, and **User Interface (UI)**. This task might feel monumental; after all, once the tool is selected we are stuck with it forever! However, as it turns out, the tool itself is the least important part of setting up a CI environment.

After all, a CI tool is nothing but a glorified cron job, with a UI attached to it. At its core, a CI tool runs on a set interval to check whether any updates were made to the code base; if changes are detected, it executes a saved script that we call test suite. We can set up a single script file on a computer, which executes on a cron and achieves the exact same results as the most expensive enterprise tool available on the market!

 A cron job is a software utility on Unix-like systems, which executes a specified task at a specified interval. Windows has an analogous utility called Task Scheduler.

It is too easy to get carried away with research and acquisition of the perfect tool that we hope will fulfill all of our needs. However, if we decouple our test suite from the CI tool, we will be able to switch tools at will. This allows us the flexibility to start with a free solution at first and migrate to a paid solution if the feature set in said solution is overwhelmingly positive.

Decoupling tests from tools

As we discussed in *Chapter 5, Stabilizing the Tests, Chapter 6, Testing the Behavior,* and *Chapter 7, The Page Objects Pattern,* our tests need to be as independent from the application and tools as possible. Decoupling tests from the implementation details of the application and reusing methods in a DRY pattern makes them easy to maintain in the long run and gives us flexibility to change things without breaking everything. The same principle applies to running our tests in CI.

To prevent a situation where we are locked into a given CI tool and cannot migrate to a better option, we need to separate the tool's tasks from the tests themselves. We will let the CI tool do what it was designed to do and nothing else. Here are the three primary functions of the CI tool:

- Looking for code changes in VCS
- Managing build node availability
- Providing some rudimentary security system to prevent accident modifications to builds

Treating the build configuration and execution with same care and respect as application code is a great way to separate the tests from the tool. Here is how we will approach the setup of the CI environment for our website:

1. Set up a separate VCS repository whose only job is to store test execution scripts.

2. Migrate any common set-up tasks, such as database migration or starting of third-party services, into the shared spaces in our VCS.

 Whether we are using Bash scripts or PowerShell scripts, it is a great idea to split different set-up tasks into functions and keep things DRY.

3. Add a script for each new job. Each script uses the shared code to set up the environment prebuild. It is the script's responsibility to trigger the build, whether it is a Rake, Maven, or Shell script.

> Some CI tools provide support for Maven, Rake, and ant builds. If we choose to use the tool's support to execute the tests, we can still use the setup scripts as part of the prebuild to configure the environment.

4. Each new build job in CI will use this repository to call the appropriate script to start the build. Since all of the setup is done within our build scripts, we no longer rely on any tool to provide all of the needed support; thus, the CI tool becomes interchangeable.

> If we are careful in the naming of build scripts in the repository to match the build name in CI, we can copy and paste the same execution commands to all of our builds and let the CI tool choose the correct script at run time.
>
> In Jenkins, the build command would look like this: `sh ${JOB_NAME}.sh`.

By separating the test execution away from the CI tool's UI, we are free to sample any tool and settle down on the one we want. The other great advantage of having a script execute our test suite is that we can execute it on our local machine without the CI. This is a great way to debug test failures that occur only when the whole suite is executed but not when we run a single test. The script will set up the database and other environment settings in an identical way to CI, thus making the illusive test failures that much easier to find.

This approach to configuring the CI job is not the only one. As you set up your own, you will find what works best for you and what does not. Whatever approach you do decide to take, just keep in mind that locking yourself into a single tool might not be the best solution in the long run, especially when you find out that the competitor's test reporting view is much more pleasing to the eye.

> I will not be listing all of the currently available enterprise and open source CI tools. Since I started working on this book, at least one more free and paid for tool was released, and many more will be released by the time you read this. Thus, a simple Internet search will provide a much better list of current tools and a feature set comparison between all of them.

Frequently Asked Questions

Even though this book is about writing tests in Selenium, most of the ideas and topics apply to test automation in general. Having said that, Selenium is not necessarily the best solution for every problem that comes along. In this section, I would like to discuss some of the most common questions I've heard asked. We will discuss each scenario, followed by problems most commonly associated with that scenario and a possible solution or possible solutions that may apply.

How to test on multiple browsers?

Testing in multiple browsers is by far the most frustrating part of working with Selenium. Certain browsers cause more problems than others by default; I'm looking at Internet Explorer. There have been multiple situations where Firefox and Chrome build would pass but Internet Explorer build will fail due to idiosyncrasies in how Microsoft decided to interpreted common web standards.

Problem

More and more web applications are hosted in Unix-like environments. Thus, the development environments are shifting away from Windows to Linux-based computers, which cannot support a local instance of Internet Explorer for quick local testing.

Possible solutions

There are multiple approaches to testing in Internet Explorer and other browsers. We will list them in order of speed and overall stability here. The first applicable choice is usually by far the best.

Localhost testing

The most reliable way to test on Internet Explorer is to have the tests execute locally on the CI node. If it is possible to add a Windows node to your CI that will execute the Selenium tests, then this is the solution for you. Having the Windows node connected to CI directly gives access to a lot of operating system level tasks that will help you make the tests stable. In the *Decoupling tests from tools* section of this chapter, we discussed a prebuild setup script that will set up the test environment. Part of that script can be terminating any orphan IE processes that may have been left over from a previous run. These orphan processes can cause a lot of environment instability for you.

Setting up Selenium Grid

Sometimes, setting up a Windows node in CI is not an option. For example, if we want to run the tests against a local instance of a website but the application stack is not compatible with Windows architecture. We will need to host the application stack on a different computer and have the Internet Explorer run against that local instance instead. This approach lacks the same amount of prebuild control; however, we discussed some possible work-around for it in the *Selenium Grid* section of this chapter.

Setting up SauceLabs Grid

Setting up a Selenium Grid might not always be the practical solution. Managing the Windows nodes is a very involved process, and having a dedicated Windows node for each version of Internet Explorer makes this even more difficult. SauceLabs takes care of hosting multiple versions of Internet Explorer and administration of the Windows nodes. The only downside is reduced performance speed, since the communication between the local instance of the website and remote browsers can become very slow. However, all of the positive features SauceLabs provides outweigh the reduction in test speed. For more information, visit the SauceLabs website at `https://saucelabs.com/`.

> SauceLabs was one of the first companies to provide Selenium nodes as a service in the cloud. Since then, several new companies started to offer this service, and the two most recent examples are Spoonium (`https://spoonium.net/`) and BrowserStack (`http://www.browserstack.com/`).

Which programming language to write tests in?

Selenium has a WebDriver implementation in every major programming language. This means that choosing the language and testing framework for your test suite should be relatively easy. You do not have to use the same language to write tests that was used to write the application itself. However, there are obvious advantages of doing so:

- **Closer integration**: If the application being tested is written on a JVM platform, it makes a lot of sense to write tests in a JVM-compatible language. This could give us closer integration with the application, making the testing effort that much easier.

Why not reuse the existing database connection object already written to query the database and find out the contents required for the test?

- **Programming help**: If you are new to programming in a given language or programming in general, never underestimate the help you can receive from the developers on your team. A single question with the right person on your team might save you days of research.

- **Developer involvement**: If the tests are written in a language developers understand and are comfortable with, they are much more willing to write and improve the tests themselves. Having a team of developers writing their own tests as they develop the feature is the best possible solution for a good quality test suite. Do not be afraid that the developers will take your job if they are also writing tests. There is always plenty to do to make sure the test suite remains stable, and you might become the Selenium guru on your team and everyone will come to you for help.

Once we have picked out the programming language and toolset we will use, we can start writing tons of new tests! At some point we will want to test on platforms and browsers other than Firefox. To help us diversify the browser coverage, let's talk about Selenium Grid.

Should we use Selenium to test the JS functionality?

Using Selenium to only test a single validation pop up on the registration page is like using a canon to kill a mosquito. However, if we review any large test suite, we will find a lot of canons used. Is Selenium the right tool to use to test a small piece of JavaScript?

Problem

Selenium is a very resource-intensive testing tool and loading the programming language, the databases, and the browser is inefficient if we are only testing JavaScript validations on a single form.

Possible solution

If we are testing the JavaScript functions on a form, we should try to isolate the code and test it by itself. There are multiple JavaScript testing tools, such as Jasmine, that allow the functions to be tested without loading the whole page. By moving the majority of tests from Selenium to Jasmine, we were able to execute 1,000+ JavaScript-only tests in under 2 minutes (4 minutes on Internet Explorer).

Jasmine is a JavaScript BDD tool that uses Selenium WebDriver to load a web browser and all of the JavaScript functions into a single page. A user writes tests in JavaScript in an RSpec-like syntax. For more information on Jasmine, visit `http://jasmine.github.io/`.

Why should I use a headless browser?

We do not need to open up an instance of Firefox to execute our Selenium tests. Having the tests run in a browser allows us to view the execution as it is happening, which helps in the writing and debugging stages of a given test. However, once the test is complete and is reliably running in CI, we don't always need to physically watch it run. A headless browser is a solution for these scenarios.

The web browser has to render the whole **Domain Object Model (DOM)** as the user navigates from page to page. The rendering is a slow and resource-intensive process. Furthermore, the operating system needs to provide a windowing service in which to render the browser. Windows can only support a single window at the time; thus, concurrent browsers end up stacking on top of each other.

Possible solution

Using a headless browser, such as HTMLUnit Driver or PhatntomJS, increases the execution speed of the test suite, since the browser is not required to render the whole DOM. Furthermore, using a headless browser is a lot less resource-intensive, allowing a higher quantity of parallel-running tests.

More information on HTMLUnit Driver can be found at `https://code.google.com/p/selenium/wiki/HtmlUnitDriver`.

PhantomJS

PhantomJS is a relatively new OSS project, which uses the WebKit engine to render web pages in memory only, and no browser window is attached. It is newer and better compared to HTMLUnit driver because it uses the actual WebKit engine instead of emulating the behavior of JavaScript. Having a real browser engine rendering the headless browser leads to much more reliable and consistent results compared to emulation.

> WebKit is a web page layout engine written by Apple for its Safari web browser. It is dramatically faster than the Trident engine used by Internet Explorer. Google has forked the WebKit project, calling it Blink engine. Currently, the Google Chrome and Opera browsers use the Blink engine.

Because PhantomJS is relatively easy to set up and the decreased suite execution time, it becomes a perfect solution for running the whole test suite on the developer's computer before committing new code to the VCS. Running a headless test suite locally and handing off the real browser execution to the real web browsers in CI can be the solution your team is looking for.

> Since PhantomJS is a relatively new project, it might not have Selenium bindings implemented for every programming language. However, the team is very active and is adding new language and frameworks all the time. For more information on PhantomJS, visit `http://phantomjs.org/`.

Which BDD tool should I use on my team?

BDD tools can provide a good starting point for any framework we want. But with so many tools to choose from, which one is the best for us?

Problem

There are multiple BDD tools available and all try to accomplish the same goal: making the functionality of the application easy to understand and decoupled from implementation. However, each tool has its own format for describing the behavior and tends to be more resource-intensive than a simpler framework. Furthermore, it might be difficult to get the whole team to agree on which description format to use; not everyone likes the *Given, When, Then* format of describing the features.

Possible solutions

If the intention of the test suite is to have a simple no frills test suite that only runs the tests without any BDD methodologies, then choosing a simple framework such as `Test::Unit` or `JUnit` might be more than sufficient. The downside is that you get what you pay for; this approach will not have all the easy-to-understand features that a BDD tool might have.

If the intended consumer of the test is from a nontechnical team, such as a project manager or manual testers, then a framework such as `Cucumber` or `JBehave` is great. It helps to specify intended behavior in clear, easy-to understand language. This is especially useful if the team uses some form of agile development methodology. The story can be directly translated into a *Given, When, Then* format. However, the tremendous amount of wordiness might not be idea for all teams.

A compromise between the preceding two options is a framework like `RSpec`. This tool provides a human-readable test description but in a much more precise and less wordy manner. This seems to be a lot more popular among purely development-minded people who might be turned off by the *Given, When, Then* style of behavior description.

> MiniTest is another tool that uses the RSpec style of feature description but is much more lightweight and faster than RSpec. MiniTest is automatically bundled with Ruby, starting from version 1.9. For more information on this tool, visit `https://github.com/seattlerb/minitest`.

In the end, it does not matter which tool is chosen as long as the test suite is growing with good reliable tests. The best tool is not the one that has the most features, but the one that everyone will use to grow and maintain the test suite.

Can I use Selenium for performance testing?

When releasing a new version of the website, we want to make sure that the new version does not perform slower than existing code. If we do not pay attention to the website performance, it will not take a long time for our fast and new website to become slow and unpleasant to use.

Problem

Technically, we can use Selenium for performance testing. However, just because we can technically do something, a question should always be nagging us at the back of our mind: should we do it? Using Selenium for performance testing is similar to using a butter knife to cut a steak; effective but unpleasant. The following factors make Selenium unsuitable for performance testing:

- **Inaccurate**: When testing page load performance, we are not testing the server response times but page load times. Even if our website is fully loaded, some asset from a third-party application might still be loading. Timing the page load times will give inflated results.

- **Testing JavaScript performance**: Selenium is not the best tool to use to test the performance of JavaScript on the page. First of all, it is too big and clumsy to give any results worth noting. Since JavaScript is technically a single-threaded language, that means that our site's scripts will have to share resources with any third-party JavaScript loaded in the browser. The slower than expected results might be coming from something outside of our control.

- **Testing asset performance**: If we cannot reliably test JavaScript performance and the performance of complete page loads, maybe we can test the asset loading. Selenium will not be able to tell you accurately how fast a certain image or video downloaded and rendered in the browser. Browser performance depends on so many factors outside of the current page, such as the amount of windows currently open, available RAM, disk usage, and CPU usage by background processes. Not to mention the asset caching performed by the browser and the caching performed by a network caching proxy that your IT department installed for the whole company. It is close to impossible to get consistent download and render time results without using Selenium.

- **Testing server load**: By far, testing the server load with Selenium is the least helpful experience. In order to generate noticeable load on the web server we need dozens, if not hundreds of Selenium instances, and even then, it might not be enough.

In conclusion, Selenium is a terrible solution for performance testing. There are simpler and better solutions available.

Possible solutions

Depending on the type of performance testing we are trying to accomplish, there are specialized tools to accomplish just about any goal. For example, to put a server under heavy load and record the response times from it, JMeter is a great tool. It simulates user behavior by recording the HTTP interactions your browser makes as you normally browse the website and replays these interactions with thousands of concurrent requests.

> For more information on the JMeter project, visit at `http://jmeter.apache.org/`.

To test the performance of the JavaScript on a given page, Google provides the V8 Benchmark Suite (`http://v8.googlecode.com/svn/data/benchmarks/v7/run.html`).

If we want to have a cross-browser solution for checking what assets are slow to load, YSlow (`http://yslow.org/`) is a great tool for that. Furthermore, most modern browsers provide a built-in test suite for JavaScript and asset performance.

Finally, if none of the tools mentioned satisfy your needs, we can write our own scripts. Using Ruby or Bash, we can write a simple script that makes HTTP requests against different API endpoints or assets and records the time it took to complete a purchase request or for an image to download. At the end of the day, a simple shell script will provide a much more accurate performance report than a Selenium test.

Summary

This concludes *Selenium Design Patterns and Best Practices*. The goal of this book was to demonstrate that Selenium testing is more than just clicking on links. To test a complicated application in a reliable and repeatable way requires a sophisticated Selenium test suite. Throughout this book, we touched upon some of the most difficult problems that I and people like myself have been encountering in the field of test automation. I hope that our collected knowledge will help save you weeks or months of frustration and confusion that I have personally experienced.

In conclusion, technical solutions provided in this book might not be the best solution in your individual case. However, I hope they will send you on the right path to something that fits perfectly for you. Improvising is a large part of this new field, so find out what works for you and share your accumulated knowledge with the Selenium community. Together, we can make test automation into an integral part of software development.

Now, go write some tests!

Getting Started with Selenium

If you are new to the Ruby programming language or new to Selenium WebDriver, there are just a couple of things you need to get your computer ready for testing. In this section, we will install some software prerequisites. At the end of the section, we will talk about Ruby class naming techniques so that it is easier to understand the test classes that we write.

Setting up the computer

There are multiple ways to develop and run Selenium WebDriver tests. Depending on the programming language you choose to use, different tools and **Integrated Development Environments (IDE)** will be available to you. In this book, we are using the Ruby programming language with the `selenium-webdriver` gem. However, this book was not intended to show how to write the most efficient Ruby programs, instead it is meant to show the best approaches to solve a given problem in general; it just happens that the examples that appear in this book are written in Ruby.

> As most proficient Ruby developers will notice, the syntax used in this book is technically correct but does not follow the standard Ruby paradigms. The Ruby code examples are deliberately overly verbose to help Ruby developers feel more at home.

All of the code and examples used for this book were chosen so that they would be as inexpensive (or free) for the reader as possible and anyone can follow the whole text with their favorite text editor of choice. This, however, means that we have to do a little work before we get started to be ready to write tests. The only prerequisites to get started are as follows:

- The Command Line Interface terminal
- The Internet connection
- The Ruby runtime environment
- The Firefox web browser
- The text editor of choice

Let's get started by adding these prerequisites to your computer.

Using Command Line Interface

The **Command Line Interface (CLI)** is one of the most powerful ways to interface with any OS. No matter what OS you have installed on your computer, you already have a powerful CLI toolset preinstalled. Let's take a look at different kinds of CLI terminals, based on the host OS.

 In the context of this book, the terms **CLI** and **terminal** are interchangeable.

Using the terminal on Windows

Microsoft Windows rarely requires the use of the terminal for day-to-day operations. Unlike Linux, most administrative tasks are completed in the **Graphical User Interface (GUI)**, that is, it requires the user to click on things with the mouse. MS-DOS CLI is available on all versions of Windows. Recently, Microsoft has made a lot of improvements to the CLI; the improved tool is called PowerShell. Finally, if you are a fan of Linux-style CLI, you can install a Linux Terminal Emulator. Either option is completely valid for the purposes of this book, so you are free to choose the option that suits you best. Let's take a closer look at each option.

Using MS-DOS

Using MS-DOS is as simple as opening the terminal and starting to interact with it. Perform the following steps:

1. To open MS-DOS, click on the **Start** button in Windows, as shown here:

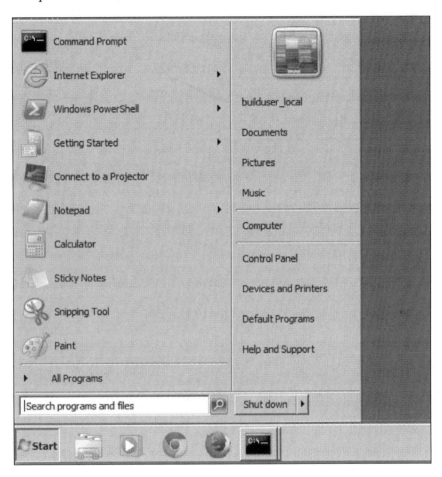

2. Locate the **Run** option application as shown here:

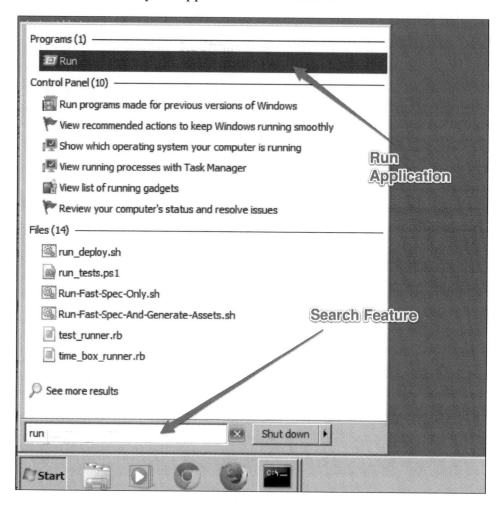

The preceding screenshot shows the Windows 7 interface, where the **Run** application is found with the search feature.

> A common Windows shortcut is to press the *Windows + R* on your keyboard.

3. Next, type in cmd in the **Run** application and hit *Enter*:

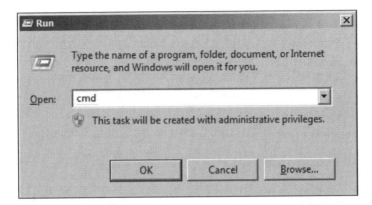

4. An MS-DOS window similar to the following one should open up:

Using PowerShell

Starting with Windows Vista, PowerShell is automatically included in the OS.

> If you are using an older version of Windows, you can download the PowerShell installer from http://technet.microsoft.com/en-us/library/hh847837.aspx.

PowerShell improves on a lot of problems that MS-DOS had, and now follows Linux's Bash style paradigm.

To open the PowerShell terminal, we will follow the same steps as shown in MS-DOS, but instead of typing in cmd, we will type in powershell. The PowerShell terminal, shown in the following screenshot, is very similar to the MS-DOS terminal:

```
Administrator: Windows PowerShell                                        _ □ ×
Windows PowerShell
Copyright (C) 2009 Microsoft Corporation. All rights reserved.

PS C:\Users\builduser_local> _
```

Using the terminal emulator

CygWin is an opensource project to bring a Linux style CLI terminal to Windows. It is a good alternative to MS-DOS. You can download the CygWin installer from the project's website at https://www.cygwin.com/.

Using the terminal on Mac OS X

Mac OS X comes with a great CLI terminal application. It runs Bash shell by default, and anyone who is comfortable with Linux shell will find himself or herself comfortably at home with Terminal.app. To start using Terminal.app, navigate to the Applications directory and open the Utilities folder.

> *Command + Shift + U* is the shortcut that will take you to the Utilities folder if you execute it within the finder.

Locate the Terminal.app and open it.

Using the terminal on Linux

To open the Terminal app in Linux, we will simply open the **Applications** menu, locate the **Accessories** option, and click on **Terminal**.

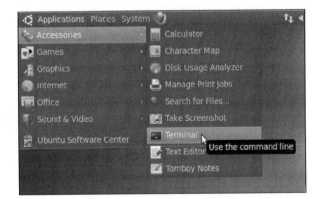

Configuring the Ruby runtime environment

Once you have found the CLI Terminal in our application, you can continue with the Ruby runtime environment installation and configuration.

Installing Ruby

Some OSes come with Ruby preinstalled, such as Mac OSX and certain distributions of Linux. We can install or upgrade our version of Ruby by finding the appropriate installer on the Ruby project's website at `https://ruby-lang.org/en/installation`.

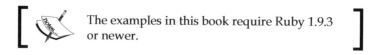 The examples in this book require Ruby 1.9.3 or newer.

Installing the selenium-webdriver gem

The Ruby runtime environment uses **Ruby gems (gems)** as a package manager for all third-party libraries. This package manager is really easy to use and contains many great features. After the Ruby runtime is installed, all we have to do to install any gem is to run the following command in the terminal:

```
gem install selenium-webdriver
```

The preceding example will install all of the dependencies that Selenium WebDriver has along with the WebDriver gem. A helpful website that can provide a lot of information for any gem is located at `http://rubygems.org`. There we can find information about the gem, such as the names of the contributors, the project's main website, all of the released versions of the gem, and any dependencies that the gem has.

Installing Firefox

We will be using the Firefox browser for all of the examples in this book. All of the examples described here will work with any other browser that WebDriver supports. However, Firefox was chosen because it needs the least amount of out of the box setup. If you do not yet have Firefox installed on your computer, download it from `http://mozilla.org`.

Understanding test class naming

Unlike Java- or C-based programming languages, Ruby does not require the filename of a class to match the class contained inside. For example, the filename `test1.rb` can contain a class named `Potato`. Furthermore, a single file can contain multiple classes within it and Ruby compiler will not complain about it. With this setup, it is very easy to loose track of different pieces of code and classes. To reduce the complexity and confusion, there are several basic rules we can follow.

Technically, these rules are more like suggestions, since the compiler will not prevent you from breaking them. Following them is advised, but not 100 percent necessary.

Naming files

It is a good idea to name the files as similar to the class that lives within it as possible. Since different test frameworks use different file naming conventions, we will adhere to the convention while at the same time clearly explaining what is contained inside the file.

For example, if we have a test that does a search for the word cheese on our website, we can name the file test_cheese_finder.rb or test_cheese_search.rb. Both examples clearly explain the intention of the test. We can still name the file test_curd_finder.rb, since it is both accepted by the compiler and expresses the intent of the test; however, not too many people will be able to find it when looking at a directory full of test files.

 Since most Ruby developers do not use an IDE, there are some common practices, such as the one described previously, to make the development simpler to accomplish.

Naming classes

Similar to naming the files, naming the test class should be done in such a way that a test failure could be understood at a quick glance. For example, in *Chapter 1, Writing the First Test*, we have an intentional test failure that looks like this:

```
Run options:

# Running tests:

F

Finished tests in 6.664776s, 0.1500 tests/s, 0.1500 assertions/s.

  1) Failure:
test_find_some_cheese(CheeseFinderTests) [cheese_finder_test.rb:13]:
Failed assertion, no message given.

1 tests, 1 assertions, 1 failures, 0 errors, 0 skips
```

By looking at the failure message, we can identify the original intention of the test by the following three clues:

- The filename of the failure tells us that the tests contained inside will be testing the ability to find `cheese` on our website, as shown in the following screenshot:

```
Run options:

# Running tests:

F

Finished tests in 6.664776s, 0.1500 tests/s, 0.1500 assertions/s.

  1) Failure:
test_find_some_cheese(CheeseFinderTests) [cheese_finder_test.rb:13]:
Failed assertion, no message given.
                                                       File name
1 tests, 1 assertions, 1 failures, 0 errors, 0 skips
```

- The class name, shown with an arrow in the following screenshot, reinforces the idea conveyed by the filename:

```
Run options:

# Running tests:

F

Finished tests in 6.664776s, 0.1500 tests/s, 0.1500 assertions/s.
                                     Class Name
  1) Failure:
test_find_some_cheese(CheeseFinderTests) [cheese_finder_test.rb:13]:
Failed assertion, no message given.

1 tests, 1 assertions, 1 failures, 0 errors, 0 skips
```

- The test method name in the following screenshot shows that this particular test was testing the positive search result. If we wanted to test for negative search results, we would have named it `test_cannot_find_cheese`.

```
Run options:

# Running tests:

F

Finished tests in 6.664776s, 0.1500 tests/s, 0.1500 assertions/s.
                          Test method name
  1) Failure:
test_find_some_cheese(CheeseFinderTests) [cheese_finder_test.rb:13]:
Failed assertion, no message given.

1 tests, 1 assertions, 1 failures, 0 errors, 0 skips
```

Understanding the namespace

Namespacing is a way of grouping logically related code together. Ruby modules are a great way to accomplish this, because they allow the declaration of classes within them. This allows us to have multiple classes with the same name within the same application without having a collision. It is similar to having two files with the same name in different directions.

When writing out the path to a class, Ruby uses the :: characters as a delimiter. For example, in *Chapter 1*, *Writing the First Test*, we are introduced to the Test::Unit framework for writing tests. All of the test classes inherit their behavior from the TestCase class in this framework. When the path to TestCase is fully written out, it looks like Test::Unit::TestCase. This statement gives us the following information:

- The TestCase class lives inside of the Unit module
- The Unit module lives within the Test namespace

Namespacing is a great way to sort our code in such a way that we can understand the intention of an object at a glance. It is similar to sorting the music collection by genre.

Showing object inheritance

The Test::Unit framework provides us with many great shortcuts when testing. For example, when we want to compare two numbers with each other and make sure they are equal, we can write our own comparison or we can use the assert method to do a comparison and display a meaningful failure message. Since we do not wish to write out every comparison by hand, we want our test class to inherit this behavior from the testing framework.

 For more information about objects, object-oriented programming, and inheritance, read *Chapter 7*, *The Page Objects Pattern*.

In Ruby, we declare object inheritance with the < character. This character shows the direction in which the inheritance is flowing; the < character shows the direction of inheritance, like an arrow. In the following test class declaration, we know that the CheeseFinderTest class will inherit all of its functionality from the TestCase class.

```
class CheeseFinderTests < Test::Unit::TestCase
```

Summary

In this section, we concluded the setup of our test machine. You also learned the location of the CLI terminal for the majority of operating systems. Also, we installed all of the necessary components that will allow us to follow all of the exercises in this book.

We also took the time to understand why our test classes are named the way they are. We covered the file and class naming conventions, and you also understand how Ruby does namespacing and declares inheritance.

We are now ready to start writing our tests!

Index

Curl 163
Cygwin
  URL 210

D

Dan North
  URL 146
data accessibility
  versus data relevance 86, 87
data relevance
  versus data accessibility 86, 87
data stubs
  using 104, 105
debug tool, Ruby 31
Decorator pattern 129
default values pattern
  about 105
  advantages 105
  and faker, merging 106
  disadvantages 106
default values pattern, merging with faker
  comment test, updating to use default
      values 108-110
  faker methods, implementing 106-108
disadvantages, Record and Playback pattern
  bad locators 10
  duplicate code 10
  hardcoded test data 10
  inflexible tests 10
  poorly written tests 10
Domain Object Model (DOM) 222
Domain Specific Language (DSL) 174
Don't Repeat Yourself (DRY) 64, 175
DRY testing pattern
  about 64, 65
  advantages 65
  code, moving into setup 66- 68
  code, moving into teardown 66-68
  disadvantages 65, 66
  duplication, removing with methods 68, 69
  external test goals, removing 69
  method used, for filling out review form 70
  refactored code, reviewing 70-72

DSL framework 174
duplication
  removing, with methods 68, 69

E

elements
  inspector window, using 44-46
  locating, on page 42, 43
end-to-end test 203
environment management
  CI environment management 209
  new builds, deploying 209
environment variables
  about 90
  setting 90
env.rb file 154
exit command 33
external test goals
  removing 69

F

failures, tests
  reasons for 59-61
faker
  and default values pattern, merging 106
faker methods
  implementing 106-108
feature files, Cucumber 150
feature growth strategy 205
File.dirname(__FILE__) call 88
files
  naming 235
Firebug
  about 44
  URL 44
Firefox
  installing 234
fixture data
  API, using as source 102-104
  parsing 92, 93
  using, in tests 93, 94
fixtures. *See* test fixtures

Thank you for buying
Selenium Design Patterns
and Best Practices

About Packt Publishing

Packt, pronounced 'packed', published its first book "*Mastering phpMyAdmin for Effective MySQL Management*" in April 2004 and subsequently continued to specialize in publishing highly focused books on specific technologies and solutions.

Our books and publications share the experiences of your fellow IT professionals in adapting and customizing today's systems, applications, and frameworks. Our solution based books give you the knowledge and power to customize the software and technologies you're using to get the job done. Packt books are more specific and less general than the IT books you have seen in the past. Our unique business model allows us to bring you more focused information, giving you more of what you need to know, and less of what you don't.

Packt is a modern, yet unique publishing company, which focuses on producing quality, cutting-edge books for communities of developers, administrators, and newbies alike. For more information, please visit our website: www.packtpub.com.

About Packt Open Source

In 2010, Packt launched two new brands, Packt Open Source and Packt Enterprise, in order to continue its focus on specialization. This book is part of the Packt Open Source brand, home to books published on software built around Open Source licenses, and offering information to anybody from advanced developers to budding web designers. The Open Source brand also runs Packt's Open Source Royalty Scheme, by which Packt gives a royalty to each Open Source project about whose software a book is sold.

Writing for Packt

We welcome all inquiries from people who are interested in authoring. Book proposals should be sent to author@packtpub.com. If your book idea is still at an early stage and you would like to discuss it first before writing a formal book proposal, contact us; one of our commissioning editors will get in touch with you.

We're not just looking for published authors; if you have strong technical skills but no writing experience, our experienced editors can help you develop a writing career, or simply get some additional reward for your expertise.

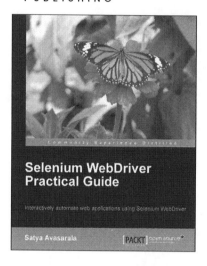

Selenium WebDriver Practical Guide

ISBN: 978-1-78216-885-0   Paperback: 264 pages

Interactively automate web applications using Selenium WebDriver

1. Covers basic to advanced concepts of WebDriver.

2. Learn how to design a more effective automation framework.

3. Explores all of the APIs within WebDriver.

4. Acquire an in-depth understanding of each concept through practical code examples.

TestComplete Cookbook

ISBN: 978-1-84969-358-5   Paperback: 282 pages

Over 110 practical recipes teaching you to master TestComplete – one of the most popular tools for testing automation

1. Learn to produce easily modifiable and maintainable scripts.

2. Customize convenient and optimal launches of created tests.

3. Explore TestComplete's possibilities and advantages through illustrative examples and code implementations.

Please check **www.PacktPub.com** for information on our titles

Robot Framework Test Automation

ISBN: 978-1-78328-303-3   Paperback: 98 pages

Create test suites and automated acceptance tests from scratch

1. Create a Robot Framework test file and a test suite.

2. Identify and differentiate between different test case writing styles.

3. Full of easy-to-follow steps to get you started with Robot Framework.

Learning Software Testing with Test Studio

ISBN: 978-1-84968-890-1   Paperback: 376 pages

Embark on the exciting journey of test automation, execution, and reporting in Test Studio with this practical tutorial

1. Learn to use Test Studio to design and automate tests valued with their functionality and maintainability.

2. Run manual and automated test suites and view reports on them.

3. Filled with practical examples, snapshots, and Test Studio hints to automate and substitute throwaway tests with long-term frameworks.

Please check **www.PacktPub.com** for information on our titles

Made in the USA
Middletown, DE
25 August 2015